"FATHER TOM" OF THE ARCTIC

By Louis L. Renner, S.J.

Binford & Mort Publishing

Portland, Oregon

FRONT COVER PHOTO:
Father Tom deplaning at Ladd Air Force Base, Fairbanks,
in the spring of 1959 after spending time on the polar ice cap.
(Fairbanks Daily News Miner photo. Oregon Province Archives)

Foreword

The history of Alaska cannot be written without the history of missionaries, who, with steadfast and singular convictions, and often with hardship, brought the Christian religion to the Native peoples. Interest in the missionary movement and the establishment of churches in Alaska has gained momentum in recent years, and the resulting articles and books have given us a better understanding of the complex web woven by the various denominations who set up camp in different places and at different times.

For the past ten years, Father Louis L. Renner, S. J., has been compiling the history of Catholic missions through a series of publications about special contributions made by Jesuit priests — some 15 so far. Two biographies are book length, *Pioneer Missionary to the Bering Strait Eskimos: Bellarmine Lafortune, S.J.*, published in 1979, and this one about Father Thomas Patrick Cunningham. Renner's articles and books, however, are more than just episodes in the lives of priests; they are also windows onto the lives of other people, with information about anthropology, geography, and the contemporary milieu. He has written them almost entirely from manuscript sources — unpublished correspondence, Jesuit house diaries, reports — and from interviews, reducing a seeming ocean of unrelated documents into compact treatises, a task which never tried can scarcely be appreciated! This is history at its most exciting level.

Fr. Lafortune introduced Cunningham to the Alaska missions, and the two priests were alike in many respects. Both were naturalized citizens, Lafortune from Quebec, the French sector of Canada, and Cunningham from New Zealand, though his Irish imagination often fantasized Ireland as his place of birth. Both were deeply attached to their Eskimo parishioners, and were involved in their lives to the extent of learning the Eskimo language; yet they did not neglect their non-Native flocks when they were in Nome or other mixed parishes, regarding them as neither more nor less important than the Eskimos. Both of them lived at what would seem to be below the poverty level on King Island (both Lafortune and Cunningham were missionaries there) and Little Diomede (where Cunningham spent eight years). This was their own choice — an uncomplaining one to be sure — as was their adoption of an Eskimo diet. But most important, neither of them, if given the chance, would have changed anything in his life.

Yet they were quite different in other ways. Although Lafortune had guided Cunningham into some of his missionary paths, his outlook on the world at large diverged. Lafortune was Catholic — first, last, and always. There was only one true way of life for him. There was no dissension in the ranks. He lived almost exclusively in his world of King Island and its 175 inhabitants and his occasional congregations on the Seward Peninsula mainland. Cunningham, on the other hand, though equally devout and true to his vows, recognized the diversities of life that created different beliefs, and had many non-Catholic friends and acquaintances. I knew Father Tom when I lived in Nome, and the name "Father Tom" as uttered by one and all seemed always to mean, "He's one of us, no matter who we are." He was just about the best advertisement that could be had for Catholicism. I have no doubt that he made converts by just being "Father Tom."

Lafortune did not leave the Seward Peninsula area from his arrival in 1903 until 1947 when illness sent him to Fairbanks where he died that year, but Cunningham was a world traveler and the most peripatetic northern missionary of his time. Although he had been infected by the wanderlust long before he became a chaplain, first in the U.S. Army, then in the U.S. Air Force, this duty developed it full-blown in wanderings that ranged all the way from Japan, Guam, Hawaii, and his old New Zealand home, to an ice floe 250 miles from the North Pole, where he worked as a consultant in arctic ice conditions for the Air Force.

Cunningham played his religious and secular roles with equal ease, but despite his wide-ranging activities and his national acclaim, he never forgot his primary vocation as a priest.

Dorothy Jean Ray

Introduction

We had just finished our evening dinner, and were sitting around in the basement recreation room of Loyola Hall in Fairbanks. Our attention was focused on one man, our honored guest, but not a stranger to our small Jesuit community. He did most of the talking; we did the listening, fascinated. It was toward mid-December 1958.

Appearing even more careworn than usual, he sat there on the sofa, wearing the Roman collar under his "Alaska Tuxedo," the greenish Filson whipcord suit so popular in Alaska at the time. Bulky white felt "bunny boots" seemed to give him disproportionately large feet. Smoke curled up from the cigarette he was holding between the middle and ring fingers of his right hand, for, as a priest, he was careful not to stain the thumb and index finger between which he daily held the consecrated host.

In his customary soft-spoken way our fellow Jesuit, "Father Tom" Cunningham, unfolded for us the dramatic events of the previous weeks, events that marked his features, made him a national celebrity, and led to his early grave.

I was especially spellbound as he talked, newcomer as I was to Alaska, and face to face with my personal "hero" for the first time. But that memorable evening at Loyola Hall was not my first contact with Father Tom. Ten years earlier he and I had exchanged letters when I proposed to spend two years with him on King Island to learn the Inupiaq Eskimo language. Both he and Francis D. Gleeson, S.J., bishop of Alaska at the time, thought my proposal a reasonable one. In Rome, however, it was an idea whose time had not yet come.

A quarter of a century has elapsed since the death of Cunningham, a man described as "one of the most loved, versatile and dynamic missionaries ever to serve the Alaska missions." His life deserved to be written long ago. As a matter of fact, four different individuals made plans to write it shortly after he died. For various reasons none of them did anything about it other than assemble biographical data. Chief among these was George T. Boileau, S.J., his close friend and Religious Superior. Immediately upon Cunningham's death, Boileau proceeded to gather materials for a biography. Letters from Cunningham's family and acquaintances in New Zealand, as well as from his many friends — especially from his military days — began to flow in. The 11th Air Division Headquarters made Cunningham's Master Personnel Records File available to

Boileau, "in view of the worldwide interest generated in Father Cunningham's past activities in the Arctic and his service to the U. S. Air Force."

Before Boileau could carry out his writing project, however, he was appointed General Superior of the Jesuits in Alaska, a position that left him little time for writing. While still Superior, he was chosen to succeed Bishop Gleeson, and less than a year after he was consecrated bishop, he died suddenly of a heart attack. The Cunningham materials he had gathered were placed in the Oregon Province Archives of the Society of Jesus, housed in the Crosby Library, Gonzaga University, Spokane, Washington.

In my research for the writing of the life of Jesuit Father Bellarmine Lafortune (Renner 1979), I kept bumping into Cunningham. It was Lafortune who first introduced him to missionary work among the Eskimos of western Alaska, and it was he who founded the mission on Little Diomede Island where Cunningham was to hold station for roughly a decade. For eleven years the two worked in a complementary partnership in the Seward Peninsula-Bering Strait area. When Lafortune died in 1947, Cunningham took his place on King Island. The Cunningham story, while not a sequel to the Lafortune story, is in many ways closely related to it.

By the fall of 1982 I had walked in Cunningham's footsteps on the Seward Peninsula, on the islands of Bering Strait, and at Barrow. Thanks to the kindness of archivist Father Clifford A. Carroll, S.J., I had the run of the Oregon Province Archives during a sabbatical leave following fifteen years as professor of German at the University of Alaska-Fairbanks. By that time I was familiar enough with my new job, editor of *The Alaskan Shepherd*, to make some slack time for free-lance writing. The Cunningham story begged to be written.

Were I to tell the reader that what follows is Cunningham's posthumous autobiography, he might assume that I wrote something I did not intend to write, or that I am simply trying to be facetious. However, there is some justification for describing the Cunningham story as quasi-autobiographical, since much of the main story consists of direct quotations from letters and diary entries written by Cunningham himself. In general, this account is based almost entirely on original, unpublished material such as letters, diaries, Cunningham-related official military papers, and personal interviews conducted by myself.

In the story that follows, these materials have often been left to speak for themselves. I felt that quoting from the sources would make Cunningham, his associates, and the milieu in which they lived more vivid than would paraphrasing.

I occasionally edited some of the material, but only slightly, and with care to insure the integrity of the original text. Not all the quotations are integral, though they may seem to be so. In some quotations, where the quoted passage has not been distorted by omissions, ellipses (. . .) have not been used.

Most of the quotations are documented by numbered references, but when the text itself contains adequate information to guide the reader to the sources, no references are given. References to the many and diverse documents dealing with Cunningham's military connections are conspicuous by their absence. All of these documents are in his archive file where they can be readily consulted.

Acknowledgements

My very sincere thanks to Fathers Wilfred P. Schoenberg, S.J., and Clifford A. Carroll, S.J., former archivists in charge of the Oregon Province Archives in Spokane, whose magnanimous support was essential to the telling of the Cunningham story. *Merci* to Père Joseph Cossette, S.J., of the Archives de la Compagnie de Jésus in Saint-Jérôme, Quebec, for providing me with important Cunningham-related materials. My thanks also to Father Provincial, Thomas R. Royce, who gave me access to the Cunningham-related correspondence in the Jesuit Provincial Archives in Portland.

I owe debts of gratitude to Père Paul de Jonghe, S.J., of Namur, Belgium, for the picture of the Jesuit house of philosophy, Eegenhoven; to J.K. Molloy of *The New Zealand Tablet* for sending me articles by and about Cunningham; and to Father Francis E. Mueller, S.J., for making available to me Cunningham's Barrow diary, as well as for reading the manuscript and making valuable suggestions. Likewise for reading the manuscript and pointing out ways of improving it significantly I thank especially Father Richard L. McCaffrey, S.J., along with Donald and Morva Hoover, and Father George E. Carroll, S.J. Thanks also to Sue Lium for verifying the exact name of Dr. Walter and for her gallant, if unsuccessful, effort to track down the full and exact name of the nurse Eliza.

The story of Father Tom would be noticeably less complete were it not for the substantial amount of information contained in letters written to me, and for personal interviews graciously granted by a large number of people interested in having the Cunningham story told. Their names appear in the notes, yet their contributions deserve to be acknowledged more explicitly. They are the following, and I want them to know me grateful: E. Anable, T. Carlin, E. Curry, W. Elliott, G. Feltes, E. Fortier, G. Gaughan, J. Gaughan, J. Hurley, L. Kaplan, M. Kelly, T. Liddy, S. Llorente, T. Martin, B. McMeel, M. Meade, H. O'Brien, F. O'Dea, R. Picard, F. Ross, H. Small, A. Walsh, and J. Walsh.

Louis L. Renner, S.J.

Contents

1 / New Zealand, Australia, Ireland, Belgium, Spokane: 1906-1930

Thomas Patrick Cunningham was born restless and preordained to a life of high adventure. He began his life's odyssey "down under" in New Zealand, where he was born, the third of four boys, to Irish immigrants Patrick Cunningham and Bridget Dwyer on February 24, 1906. His mother died when he was four years old, and his father remarried two years later. The boy Tom inherited an intense, lifelong affection for his ancestral land from his father.[1]

New Zealand's lush, rolling, green countryside, speckled white with great herds of sheep, served the Cunninghams well as a substitute land for the pastoral tranquility of old Ireland. But the Cunninghams were dairy farmers, not sheepherders. On their farm of approximately 100 acres near Mosgiel in East Taieri, Otago, South Island, they milked daily — by hand — 30 to 40 cows, a chore shared by all of the Cunningham family.

For some years the Cunningham children and those of a family named Flannery — the only Catholic families in the area — attended a state school at Wyllie's Crossing, a small settlement near their farms, three miles from Mosgiel. In this small school of only about 30 pupils, the Cunninghams and Flannerys would often be ignored — not even spoken to — because they were Catholics. Tom Cunningham and Theresa Flannery always walked home from school together. She wrote many years later, "I well remember Fr. Tom — always the gentleman — would carry my schoolbag for me." Tom's older brother John wrote, "His childhood was uneventful. He was always full of life, and ready for fun."[2]

1

Mosgiel, Taieri Plain, Otago, New Zealand, where Thomas Cunningham was born and spent his boyhood years. *(Oregon Province Archives)*

Finding the religious atmosphere at the Wyllie's Crossing school unsuitable for Tom, his parents decided to have him finish his primary education at the convent school in Mosgiel, which meant a daily six-mile round trip on foot for the boy. Next he attended the Christian Brothers High School in Dunedin, a city ten miles from Mosgiel, commuting daily by train. He completed his pre-Jesuit education by attending Holy Cross College, the diocesan seminary, in Mosgiel from 5 March 1921 to December 1923.[3] On 4 March 1924, he was received into the Irish Province of the Society of Jesus in Sydney, Australia. (Australia was at this time a dependent Mission of the Irish Province.) Although there were no Jesuits in New Zealand, the boy Tom very likely had learned about them from books and mission magazines, and from his parents, who knew them in Ireland.

After completing his two years of novitiate in Sydney, and vowing perpetual poverty, chastity, and obedience in the Society of Jesus, Cunningham sailed to Ireland toward the end of August 1926, for a year of classical studies at Rathfarnham Castle, the Jesuit "Juniorate" near Dublin.

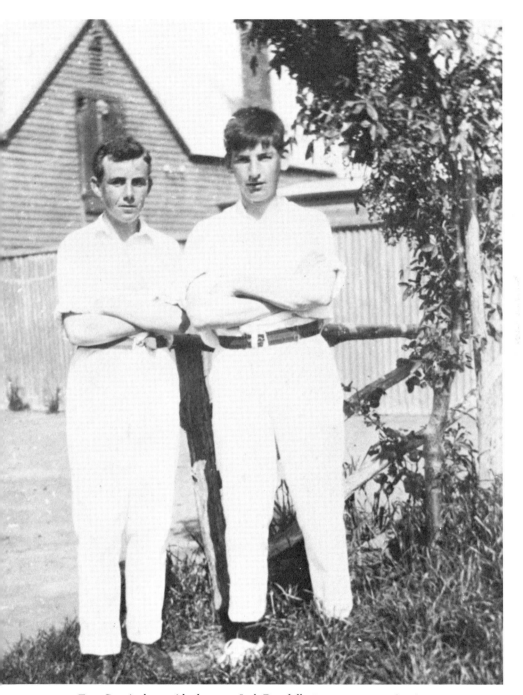

Tom Cunningham with classmate Jack Dowdall. *(Oregon Province Archives)*

During that year in Ireland he and his fellow "Juniors" received heavy, almost daily dosages of Latin and Greek, history and English literature. But there was also relief from the rigid, semi-monastic, quasi-military academy routine in holydays and holidays, and in work and recreation periods, with occasional excursions into the relaxing, bucolic Irish countryside. Several of his classmates have left accounts of his doings at this time.

Rathfarnham Castle much as it looked during Cunningham's year there. *(Photo courtesy of Matthew Meade, S.J.)*

"He often astounded us," wrote one, "by doing spine-chilling feats like climbing rickety radio poles on towering buildings with a nonchalance that was unbelievable. There is a well-known lake up in the mountains about thirty miles from Dublin. The water in it is bitterly cold even in the summer. Tradition has it that St. Kevin lived on a cleft high up on one side of its sheer cliffs. Father Tom went with a party in a boat one day over to those cliffs, climbed up to Kevin's hideout and dived into the chill waters 30 to 40 feet below! The boatmen on the lake still tell visitors of their horror when they saw him plunge down."[4]

Another wrote that Cunningham "was a great swimmer, and delighted in daring diving. Apparently he loved the challenge of deeds demanding courage and endurance." And still others wrote that "he had a great sense of humour, and was always very happy in himself," and that he "was very popular with everyone on account of his sincere openness and readiness to help in manual projects such as carpentry...He was a strong Irishman and used to nail an Irish flag to his room door every year on St. Patrick's Day. He always sympathized with the underdog."[5]

Toward the end of his stay in Ireland, Cunningham wrote to his paternal aunt, Margaret Mahoney of New York City, on 15 September 1927, "I like [Ireland] very much and am sorry to be leaving it so soon." On 17 September 1927, after visiting closely related Cunninghams in Ballylongford, he left Ireland for philosophical studies at the Jesuit college at Eegenhoven, located four miles from Louvain, Belgium.

En route to Eegenhoven he spent three nights in London, one in Bruges (which struck him as "a rather old, dirty town, but has a couple of splendid churches"), and one in Brussels, a "very beautiful" town, he wrote to his parents, "and the boulevards and splendid clean buildings make it look very much like Paris." In Brussels he and his companions had a swim in the open-air baths, just to keep themselves in "good trim."

When Cunningham arrived at the Jesuit college, he found a community of 139 Jesuits, housed in a new building surrounded by a large farm.

The Jesuit house of philosophy, Eegenhoven, Belgium, before the fire of 1940. *(Centre de Documentation et de Recherche Religieuses, Namur, Belgium)*

"The lads were just getting along to dinner," he wrote. "They are a rather mixed lot — Belgian, German, Hungarian, French, Czechoslovakian, Irish."[6] The official language of the house was French, which he had studied in school and could understand if it was spoken slowly. There were only five native English speakers in the community.

Cunningham found the food at Eegenhoven to be "a bit strange, but it tastes much better than it looks." The one dish he had difficulty getting used to at first was buttermilk soup. Beer and wine were served at all the meals. "I would give a fortune," he wrote, "for a sup of 'rale tay.' "[7]

By the end of October, he was getting used to even buttermilk soup, and was able to "surround the other peculiar concoctions that they turn out. It isn't so much the grub itself, but the way they cook it. You have to go easy on the first couple of mouthfuls until you get into your stride, so to speak."[8]

At this time Cunningham seems to have had a touch of homesickness. From his "Mum and Dad," as he always addressed his parents, he requested photos of the family and "any photos of life down on the farm," as well as an occasional page out of the *Otago Daily*. However, he assured them that once he got used to the "grub" and the language, he would be able to survive what he anticipated would be "three years of penal servitude."[9]

The Feast of Christ the King was celebrated in Catholic Belgium with great solemnity. In some areas the national flag was flown on that day. Cunningham, to add his own version of solemnity to the occasion, hung a small Irish flag out of his window. "The lads here," he wrote home, "thought the idea quite original."[10]

Six weeks into his philosophical studies, he was finding life "pretty quiet and inclined to be a bit monotonous," and the studies "pretty hard. The stuff needs a lot of thinking." He could by now carry on a conversation in French easily enough, but he still had difficulty following the lectures, whether held in French or in Latin. "They have a very queer way of pronouncing Latin," he wrote. Studies and the constant struggle with these two languages — along with Flemish, which he was trying to learn well — brought on headaches for the first time in his life. For relief and recreation he played soccer three times a week — "just the thing to get you fresh" — and soon developed the reputation of being a good player.[11]

Twice a week the young philosophers were allowed to take recreational walks, which consisted of "walking out in your soutane, with a flat-topped parson's hat, and sometimes an umbrella hung on your arm. You walk anywhere about the roads, talking about philosophy or the lives of the saints. If you stop in [stay at home], you can play football [soccer], and that is more in my line."[12]

On Thursdays Cunningham walked to nearby Louvain to visit a fellow Irishman in the Jesuit house of theology. The two of them kept one another posted on the latest Irish political news. A priest in Ireland regularly sent Cunningham the current newspaper, his way of thanking him for the haircuts Cunningham had given him the previous year. "Up de Valera!" wrote the priest on the top of the newspaper, which, of course, received Cunningham's hearty endorsement, since he held de Valera in the highest regard. Cunningham found the people at Eegenhoven very interested in Ireland and its political struggles, and claimed that after two months he had made them all republicans, and convinced that de Valera was the man of the hour.[13]

Cunningham wrote on 20 November to his parents that the winter was beginning to get "a bit severe. The winds are terribly cold." However, the recently built Jesuit house of philosophy was well heated, and each room had a large hot water radiator. "When you lie back and put your feet up on it, it's homey enough. Of course, a fire would be much more to the point, but I suppose we must be thankful for small mercies."[14]

The 21-year-old Cunningham seems to have been in splendid physical condition at that time, writing to his Mum and Dad that he was in "tiptop form." By measuring and weighing himself he determined that he was five feet, eight and a half inches tall "in stocking soles," that he was thirty-eight inches around the chest, and that he weighed 12.3 stone [ca. 172 pounds]. His collar size he gave as seventeen inches.[15]

Cunningham was an expert marksman, a talent he put to use at Eegenhoven where rabbits were rare enough to make a rabbit pie a luxury, yet plentiful enough to cause considerable damage in the Jesuits' garden. To Cunningham's delight, the rector of the college bought him a breechloader to keep them under control. In Ireland, too, Cunningham had been provided with a gun — to keep the crows in check. "You needn't worry," he reassured his parents, "about my shooting myself. I think I have the Cunningham tradition of looking after myself." He was an expert marksman all his life. During his third year of philosophy, he was able to hit a cigarette butt at thirty yards. "That's not bad," he wrote.[16]

It was the custom for the Irishmen at Eegenhoven to "celebrate St.

Pat's Day strictly according to the established traditions." If the day fell on a Sunday, it was celebrated the following Monday, "as what's the use," asked Cunningham rhetorically, "of having St. Pat's Day at all if we don't miss a couple of philosophy lectures and a few hours study?"[17]

In 1928, for St. Patrick's Day, Cunningham and the other two Irishmen in the community managed to get some shamrock for the feast. However, he had "a little scruple about wearing it, as it had come from Belfast. Anyhow, it was better than none." On the eve of the feast, he preached in the refectory to the whole community, his remarks aimed primarily at the 14 who understood English. "I didn't go behind the bush," he wrote his parents, "to tell them what I thought of England, the Free State, De Valera, etc."[18] Thomas Patrick Cunningham was green Irish to the marrow of his bones.

On the saint's day itself, the three sons of St. Patrick were free of classes, so — after Cunningham had hung the Irish flag out of his window — they took "a nice spin through the country." They visited a monastery near Namur, where the monks showed them a "royal time" — serving them dinner, and insisting they "drown St. Patrick and the shamrock with a little nip of whiskey." Cunningham found the monastery grounds splendid, "but everything had a solemn monastic look, even the cows."[19]

For his second St. Patrick's Day at Eegenhoven, Cunningham's aunt Margaret in New York sent him a big cake. The sons of Erin, numbering six by that time, got through it in one afternoon — "and all had bad dreams that night." However, before going off to bed to have those dreams, the six "kept cheerful enough, and gave out 'The Soldiers' Song' with great gusto, just at 9:30 p.m. When just starting the third verse, a chap came up from two storeys down and told us sarcastic-like that the Irish National Anthem was a powerful song when heard even from a distance, and so late at night. I shut the door in his face," wrote Cunningham.

The Irishmen never invited any of the Englishmen to their parties. "These chaps have to be kept in their places, and we keep them well in their own back yard. They daren't open their mouths about Ireland, though I can see they are itching to do so at times."[20] Excluding the Englishmen was purely a political matter, not selfishness. During his Alaskan years Cunningham became notorious for sharing and giving things away — at times with total disregard for his own basic needs.

Cunningham took his philosophical studies seriously enough, but he was clearly not a professional philosopher in the making. Had he been, he would have taken advantage of his friendship with the renowned Belgian philosopher, Joseph Maréchal, who was writing and lecturing in Louvain at that time, to discuss philosophy. Instead, "Maréchal, the great intellectual, to cheer him up used to talk 'horses' to him."[21]

Two weeks before the 1928 Easter holidays, he wrote home that he was really looking forward to a break from the academic routine, as he was "tired of studying the why and wherefore of everything," and "about done up with study." Nevertheless, he still had a 25-page composition to write on "the driest of subjects, 'knowledge.'"[22]

Despite the disparaging comments about his studies, he had been chosen to defend a philosophical thesis in an hour-long public disputation held in Latin several weeks earlier. This was decidedly an honor for him, and an indication that he was making good progress in philosophy and was reasonably fluent in Latin.

Twice during his second year at Eegenhoven, Cunningham gave "lantern-lectures," one on "a trip to Australia," using 80 slides sent him by the Orient Company. He prepared it well beforehand, "putting in plenty of jokes. The whole circus turned out a great success, so I am making a name for myself as a lecture-giver."[23] As will be seen, Cunningham proved to be a very popular lecturer later in his career.

"I speak so well now," he wrote toward the end of his second year at Eegenhoven, "that some people take me for a Belgian. Still, I don't get out of a certain twang peculiar to English; and the sounds of Flemish and French aren't nice when you speak with a voice that seems to be coming from a chap with his head in a barrel."[24]

As a seminarian, and later on as a missionary in Alaska, Cunningham attached much importance to the learning and proper speaking of foreign or indigenous languages. During his two years at Eegenhoven, he strove to more or less master French and Flemish, as well as to achieve a certain fluency in Gaelic, which he practiced with his Irish classmates, who used it not only for patriotic reasons, but also to share secrets when in the presence of their English-speaking colleagues. Throughout his life he took pride in the fact that he never lost the Irish brogue he had acquired as a young man, and that strangers took him to be from the "auld sod" rather than from "down under."

The first indication of Cunningham's interest in Alaska is in a letter of 22 April 1929 from J. Sullivan, General Superior of the Australian

Mission (to which Cunningham still belonged), to Joseph M. Piet, the Father Provincial of the California Province of the Society of Jesus, which had charge of the Alaska Mission at that time. "There is a young scholastic [Thomas Cunningham] belonging to this Mission who is anxious to go to the Alaska Mission...As far as I know him, he seems very suitable for Mission work, being very practical, able to turn his hand to any kind of work, carpentry, etc. I do not think he has very special talent for studies, but is not dull." Piet cabled his answer the day he received Sullivan's letter, on 30 May: "Scholastic accepted. Have him arrange immediate entrance to States."

In 1959, Cunningham explained to the Women's Sodality of Elmendorf Air Force Base near Anchorage how he came to spend nearly 25 years in Alaska. "My coming to Alaska," he told the women sodalists, "was purely voluntary. When I was halfway through my course of studies, this letter came out from Rome asking for volunteer priests for Alaska and China. There was an Irishman there with me at the time, and he and I got together, and we figured the Church could not possibly get along in either country unless we volunteered. So he volunteered for China, and I volunteered for Alaska. We wrote letters accepting that night, and we mailed them. And you know, how — very often — what looks like a good idea before you go to bed, is kind of blue around the edge in the morning. Anyhow, we were accepted."[25]

Although Cunningham obviously made his decision to volunteer for Alaska rather abruptly (his letters from Eegenhoven consistently indicated that he expected to spend three years there, then return to Australia to teach), he seemed pleased with his decision, for he wrote to his Mum and Dad, "I danced around the room, when I got the letter telling me that I could go to Alaska. The night before I left, I think I was the happiest chap at Louvain."[26]

Cunningham arrived at Mount St. Michael's, the Jesuit house of philosophy on the outskirts of Spokane, Washington, on 1 October 1929, and soon impressed all with his "friendliness, his wit and humor — and his ability to kick a soccer ball with either foot through the goal posts."[27]

Only a few weeks after his arrival at "the Mount," he found himself involved in more work than he had ever thought himself capable of. In addition to attending to the ordinary class work, he led a debate, edited a special Christmas newspaper, and wrote a play for Christmas, *Box and Cox* — "a very pleasant presentation," according to a classmate who saw it. To his parents he wrote, "It's a wonder I'm not worn away to a shadow; but, Uncle Sam always supplies things well in the grub line."[28]

He did, however, find several deficiencies in the "grub line." He missed the Belgian beer for which he had acquired a taste while at Eegenhoven, "but," he consoled himself, "there is always water. Adam had to be satisfied with that." And he had difficulty developing a taste for canned meat — to which he attributed that "tinned-meat expression peculiar to Yanks."[29]

The Jesuit house of philosophy, Mount St. Michael's, Spokane, much as it looked in 1930.
(Oregon Province Archives)

"Miserable weather and a heap of work, and being among a crowd of strangers with no one to go and grumble to" left Cunningham feeling "pretty blue" as his first year in America wore on. He found the "Yanks splendid fellows"; still, he was a stranger among them. A couple of times he felt like walking to Vancouver, British Columbia, and signing on with the first ship to sail for New Zealand. "But, it was only temporary madness. I got over it pretty quick."[30]

After six months at the Mount he was gradually getting used to American ways. He found welcome relief from the unrelenting study and lecture grind in winter sports — ice skating, skiing, tobogganing — and in

swimming, just as soon as the ice was off the outdoor pool. He missed
none of the monthly in-house movies, and there was a relaxing outing
to the Mount's villa on Twin Lakes in Idaho to work on a motorboat.
When the work was finished, he "got a gun and went shooting grizzly
bears. But it was a day off for the bears — in fact, for any shooting
material — so I had to amuse myself firing at a target on the trunk
of a tree." He liked the fact that when on walks he did not have to
wear the "clerical costume" as he did in Belgium. "This makes us much
more free," he wrote his parents.[31]

Cunningham considered Rugby child's play compared to American
football. He conceded, however, that football was not quite as brutal
as it appeared, for the players wore "plenty of armour." At Mount St.
Michael's only touch football was played, and a classmate who played
with Cunningham described him as "a rather fiery, competitive athlete."[32]

Certain ways of the Yanks — especially those of doctors — still struck
him as somewhat strange. He felt, for example, that the American doctor
was much too eager to operate. "If you say you are generally run down,
he will say 'excuse me,' and go into the next room and start greasing
a saw." When Cunningham was getting his passport in Antwerp, the
American doctor there tapped him on the chest for about ten minutes,
and then put his head down and listened as if expecting to hear someone
say "come in!"[33]

As early as April, 1930, Cunningham learned that he was to go to
Alaska, a decision that had been left up to him, for he had asked to
go at the first opportunity. "Take a life-saver!" he wrote his parents
on the 7th. "I am off to Alaska in August." Normally he would have
gone to Alaska only after he had taught in some high school in the
California Province for several years, and then have studied theology
prior to ordination to the priesthood. By going early, at that time, he
felt he would be able to get a start on the Eskimo language, learn how
to train a dog team, and get used to eating fish.

Toward the end of April he received his Bachelor of Arts degree,
and on May 16th, 17th, and 19th, received the tonsure constituting him
a cleric, and the minor orders of porter, lector, exorcist, and acolyte
at the hands of Bishop Charles D. White of Spokane. Under date of
1 June the Mount diarist recorded, "7:15, movie *Thunder* in honor of
Mr. Cunningham who is going to Alaska," and the next day Cunningham took the hour-long comprehensive oral philosophy examination
in Latin. He left Mount St. Michael's on 5 June.

2 / Holy Cross, Alaska: 1930-1931 Montreal: 1931-1935

The Rev. Mr. Thomas Patrick Cunningham sailed from Seattle in July, 1930, for Seward, Alaska. From there he took the train to Fairbanks, and then a sternwheeler downriver to Nulato where he spent five weeks helping the resident missionary build a new house. "I did some solid work on that house," he wrote, "and if cold gets in there, I don't know what to think."[1] After installing electric lights in the new residence, he proceeded down the river to Holy Cross.

Holy Cross Mission on the Yukon River as it appeared in 1931. *(Photo by Bernard R. Hubbard, S.J. Courtesy of Archives University of Santa Clara)*

When, on 7 September 1930, Cunningham stepped ashore at Holy Cross Mission on the lower Yukon River in western Alaska, the mission was still in full flower. Aloysius Robaut, S.J., who had founded it in 1888, was still living as a member of the community. He had chosen this spot on the right (west) bank of the river opposite the old Native village of Koserefsky, because he thought it ideally suited for a centrally located mission and, at the same time, a boarding school for Eskimo and Indian children. The site was protected against the icy winds out of the north by a high bluff, and low, wooded hills sheltered it on the west. The mighty Yukon flowed past it on the east, and forests, dotted here and there with tundra lakes, lay to the south.

From the outset the mission was intended to be mostly self-sufficient: to provide its own lumber and firewood, and to rely on salmon from the river, game from the surrounding country, meat from its reindeer herd, and produce from its great gardens to feed its staff — Sisters of St. Ann and Jesuit priests and lay brothers — and the approximately 165 children under its care. The gardens at Holy Cross were exceptionally productive, and soon after its founding the mission was known far and wide as "the garden spot of the Yukon."[2]

For information about Cunningham and his year at Holy Cross we have to rely almost entirely on the mission's house diary. His name appears in the diary for the first time on 13 September 1930: "digging potatoes with the tractor manned by Mr. Cghm." This tractor and other machinery were to occupy many of his days at Holy Cross. "I had to work all the machinery myself. I was in my element," he wrote.[3]

On 24 September, Cunningham and Raphael, his 18-year-old Eskimo companion, left Holy Cross on the mission boat for Marshall, a village about 150 miles downriver, where they were to transfer some goods destined for Nome to another boat. Ten miles above Marshall they ran up on a sandbar and were stranded for three days and three nights. It was only with the aid of strong cables that they finally got off, returning to Holy Cross on the 30th. "Mr. Cghm and Raphael almost starve on bar," recorded the diarist that day.

From October second to the ninth, Cunningham made his annual eight-day retreat; and on the tenth, he and the older boys began to haul firewood for the 52 mission stoves, which consumed upwards of 400 cords of wood per winter. The weather was too poor for hauling wood on the 12th, so he helped wallpaper the chapel. On the 13th, according to the diary, he put his marksmanship to a test: "Old bull

'Mr. Cunningham' and Brother Hugo Horan, S.J., on the Caterpillar 15, at Holy Cross Mission, Alaska, winter 1930-1931. *(Oregon Province Archives)*

shot by Mr. Cghm...Mr. Cghm took group of boys to meadow to rake hay," and on the 21st, "Mr. Cghm made trail with tractor to new hauling place."

On 7 December, he accompanied Father Giovanni Lucchesi, S.J., on a dog-sled trip to Paimiut, an Eskimo village 22 miles southwest of Holy Cross. Keeping the tractor running and hauling firewood and logs for the sawmill occupied most of his winter days at Holy Cross. He spent the entire day of 16 December overhauling the tractor, a Caterpillar 15, and by the next day it was "functioning perfectly."

On 1 January 1931, according to the diary, "Movie in evening went off very well due to effort of Mr. Cghm," but on the following day

T. Cunningham with one of Father Bernard Hubbard's dogs, Holy Cross, 1931. *(Hubbard photo HCM-31-362n. Courtesy of Archives University of Santa Clara)*

Cunningham was "sickly" and unable to work. On 15 January, "Mr. Cghm entertained 2 Sisters and about 20 girls with radio music," and at supper, on the 23rd, he read his translation of a letter written in Latin by the Father General to the whole Society of Jesus.

During the last two days of January and the first part of February,

Cunningham spent most of his working hours wiring the house of the Fathers. Later on, after finishing a similar "excellent piece of work in Sisters' house," he wired the hospital and the boys' house. On 21 August with the help of Brother John Hess, S.J., he set up an electric plant in the basement of the Fathers' house, and "at 7 p.m. surprised the community by turning on the current. The house was fully illuminated and the engine ran with hardly any noise, no vibration, and no odor through the house. Mr. Cghm deserves a good deal of credit and praise for the work he accomplished."

By mid-May the frost was pretty well out of the ground, and Cunningham began to plow and disc the gardens and fields with the tractor for spring planting. When the salmon began to run up the Yukon in June, he took Father Paul C. O'Connor, S.J., in one of the mission boats to say Mass at the various fish camps. On 15 June, he was assigned to serve as first mate on the *Little Flower*, one of the mission boats, when it set out on a trip downriver, destination Hooper Bay Mission on the Bering Sea. Occasionally he took time out to hunt, or to hitch up and run the dogs.

But Cunningham's busy routine did not consist entirely of manual labor. From the diary we learn that he also took part in spiritual functions: "Way of the Cross by Mr. Cghm"; "Mr. Cghm gives a very nice little sermon on St. Patrick. No wood hauled, in honor of St. Patrick"; "Mr. Cghm reads Passion"; "Mr. Cghm subdeacon." But nothing indicates that he learned much Eskimo while at Holy Cross, possibly because there were few Eskimo adults there, and the children were both Eskimo and Indian.

On 24 September 1931, a little over a year after he first landed at Holy Cross, Cunningham took passage on the *Alice*, with Montreal and theological studies his ultimate destination. He had expected to spend three years at Holy Cross, and as late as April, 1931, the *Irish Province News* wrote that he was "doing excellent work in Alaska; will be most likely prefect and principal of a high school next year." Apparently his Superiors rushed him on to theology and the priesthood because of the shortage of priests in Alaska at the time.

At Montreal Cunningham devoted most of his time to the study of theology after his first year, except for his weekly catechism classes for children. That he was not much of a theologian is evident from the official record of his grades; he passed most of his examinations with an average ranking of no more than "satisfactory."

Cunningham spent July and August 1933 in northern Ontario, moving widely throughout a region he described as "the country between lake Huron and Hudson Bay." The Superior of the Indian missions there had invited him to spend his vacation with him. "I accepted," he wrote to his parents on 16 September, "thinking I would only have to stroll around with my hands in my pockets, looking at Indians, and leading a sort of 'gentleman of leisure' life. I was sadly mistaken. I put in two months of solid work; very interesting, however, and just the kind to make the muscles strong."

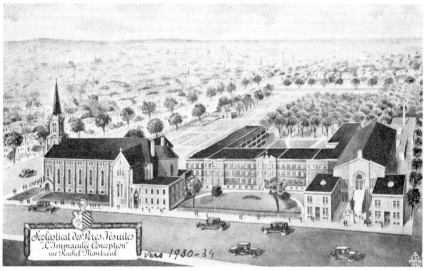

The Jesuit house of theology, 'The Immaculate Conception,' Montreal, in the early 1930s. *(Archives de la Compagnie de Jésus, Province du Canada-français)*

One of his jobs was to operate the 20-ton mission boat to haul supplies to the different missions. After satisfying government authorities that he was capable of handling the boat safely, he was given engineer's papers and a captain's permit, which qualified him to transport as many as 60 children at a time from various points to the mission school at Spanish. When not hauling freight or children, he operated the three electric generators and the sawmill at the mission.

He also wrote to his parents on 16 September that "all in all, I am keeping as fit as a fiddle; not perhaps as heavy as I might be, but still able to hold my own in a free-for-all — of which there were quite a few during the summer. Of course, age is beginning to tell." He had by now attained the ripe old age of 27 years!

'The young Father Tom.' (Oregon Province Archives)

Cunningham was ordained to the priesthood on 12 August 1934, after his third year at Montreal, but only after a few "tight squeezes," one of which was related by Joseph P. Logan, S.J., who said that he had it directly from Cunningham himself:

"One day, during his theology years at Montreal," according to Logan, "Tom felt an irresistible urge to get out for a break. He sneaked out and went downtown for an evening movie. In the course of the show, there was a scream, and an outraged woman claimed that somebody had snatched her purse. Immediately the lights went on, and the theater manager began systematically to question the patrons. He came to Tom, asked for an ID. Of course, he had none. Nor did he want to reveal his true identity. But he saw himself in a tight spot in any case, so he told him who he was, Thomas Cunningham from the theologate. This seemed so far-fetched, that he was taken for an impostor. He insisted he was who he said he was. Then he told the manager to call the theologate and ask them if there was not a student there by the name of Thomas Cunningham. The theater phoned. The Superior of the theologate agreed that there was a student there by that name, but it surely couldn't be the man in the theater, since Thomas Cunningham was in his bed long since, asleep. He hung up. The manager confronted Tom with the findings. Tom kept insisting he was who he said he was, and to phone again and check his bed. The check was made, and, sure enough, it was found empty. Incognito no longer, Tom hastened back to the theologate to face the midnight music. Given the climate of the time in Jesuit houses of study, especially in conservative French-Canada, this was more than a peccadillo. Yet, Tom, used to getting out of tight squeezes, was able to work himself out of that one too. He was ordained on schedule."[4]

One of Cunningham's three souvenir ordination cards shows a priest standing before an altar out-of-doors on a small rise and elevating the host before kneeling peasants. A farmer is seen nearby working in a field. The text below the picture is from Luke 4/18, and true to the Cunningham style, it is in Gaelic: "The Spirit of the Lord is upon me because he has anointed me; to bring good news to the poor he has sent me, to heal the contrite of heart."

Years later, he wrote to friends that "I had no one there [at his ordination]. After breakfast on the ordination day, I went out and sat under a tree and read the breviary, and there was no fuss or bother that day or the next." His memory must have failed him, for we know that all of his Mahoney relatives — uncle, aunt, cousins — were there, and that he spent the week after his ordination with them in New York.[5]

Cunningham, as a "fourth-year Father," sometimes helped out in some parish or other on the weekends. Erwin J. Toner, S.J., who had studied with him and had intended to write his biography, told about one of these weekend occasions: "Father Tom was on the train, returning to Montreal. At the opposite end of the car in which he was riding sat a foulmouthed, somewhat tipsy fellow, shooting his mouth off about priests. This he did in a voice loud enough for all in the car to hear, but especially for the benefit of Father Tom. After a bit, Father Tom could take it no longer, so he got up, went back to where the guy was sitting, and asked, 'Does that go for me too?' 'Ya-ah, dat goes for you too!' 'Get up!' he told the guy. The guy got up, and with his left Father Tom grabbed him by the chest, and with his right he smashed him one straight to the jaw that laid him out in the aisle. The people in the car cheered, and gave Father Tom a generous round of applause."[6] Cunningham had no tolerance for foul language, and more than once in his life confronted it with direct, decisive action.

Cunningham was "a spirited and very popular member of our community," according to Robert Picard, S.J., who was at Montreal with Cunningham from 1932 to 1935. "He never was the intellectual type, but, being of a practical turn of mind and highly skilled with his hands, he was always busy helping others and creating useful paraphernalia. He was quite proficient in French, and got along very well with the most nationalist Quebeckers. I remember him giving us a lecture in French in 1935, with a two-reel film taken by himself during his regency [his year at Holy Cross], on the hard life of missionaries in Alaska."[7]

3 / Nome: 1935-1936

In 1935 Cunningham's first Alaskan assignment as a priest was that of pastor of St. Joseph's Church in Nome. The Nome parish, established in 1901, had by that time seen the coming and going of 18 priests.

Holy Cross Hospital, built in 1906, rectory and St. Joseph's Church Nome. The rectory and church were built in 1901. During Cunningham's years in the Nome area these three buildings still appeared as they do in this early photo. *(Oregon Province Archives)*

Some were unsuited for work in that parish and should never have been assigned to it in the first place, but the majority were reasonable choices for the former gold-rush city on the Bering Sea. Their short tenures were due less to their inadequacies than to the formidable challenge facing any person who would venture to be pastor in Nome. Its remoteness, its frontier atmosphere and mentality, its harsh weather conditions, its disharmonious mixture of Eskimos and whites all added up to a burden greater than most priests could bear for more than a year or two. By 1935 Nome had long since been on the decline, and the only reason it continued to exist seemed to be the fact that it had existed. The momentum of its past history carried it on.[1]

Father Bellarmine Lafortune, S.J., pioneer missionary to the Bering Strait Eskimos, in 1937. *(Photo by Bernard R. Hubbard, S.J. Alaskan Shepherd collection)*

Cunningham arrived in Nome on the *S.S. Derblay* on 3 September 1935. He was originally announced for Kotzebue, but before Bellarmine Lafortune, S.J., (already a living legend in the Nome-Bering Strait area) left for his post on King Island, he informed Cunningham that he was to be pastor of the Nome parish for the coming year.[2]

In the Nome diary Cunningham recorded his first official act as pastor, the burial of Mrs. Anna Lupp, an Alaskan pioneer, long-time cook in the Nome jail, and a very devout and generous parishioner.

Early in October he organized and taught regular catechism classes. The lower grades came on Monday and Thursday afternoons at 2:30, the upper grades on Wednesday and Friday afternoons at 3:30, and the high school students at 7:00 p.m. on Mondays and Thursdays. From 6:30-8:00 p.m. on Tuesdays, Wednesdays, Fridays and Saturdays he taught the Native children in Eskimo, to the extent that his limited knowledge of that language allowed.[3] (During his Nome year he devoted four hours daily, except Sundays, to the study of Eskimo, so that in February, 1936, he could write, "I find myself making quite satisfactory progress," and by March, "The language is no longer the illogical puzzle it used to be."[4]) He recorded in the Nome diary that "all the children come very faithfully," no doubt a tribute to his gift as a storyteller who drew and held his young audiences.

Cunningham spent a week in Kotzebue in early February, 1936, at the repeated invitation of the pastor, Francis M. Ménager, S.J., and the previous suggestion of Lafortune. "The more I saw of Kotzebue," he wrote to Bishop Joseph R. Crimont, S.J., on the 26th, "the more I felt disappointed at having had my status changed." By this time he had discovered that Nome was "no picnic." He wrote to Crimont, "The cattle towns back home in N.Z. were models of virtue compared with Nome."

At Kotzebue Cunningham and Ménager discussed at length "the painful topic of Wainwright," where, they concluded, in a letter to Crimont, the Catholic Church could still "get a good hold...The Natives are very dissatisfied with the Native preacher and repeated requests are being sent to Kotzebue, and even to here [Nome], to have us open up there next summer. So, say the word and I will go up and build the church, and Fr. Ménager will be its first enthusiastic pastor." Crimont, however, did not say the word, and Cunningham had to wait a few more years before he was able to answer the call of the Arctic. Ménager noted Cunningham's visit in the Kotzebue diary: "Father Tom Cunningham was here from Nome and pleased everyone."

On 27 February, Cunningham, in a plane piloted by Chester Brown, took Martha Neuman, a Nome girl, to Holy Cross Mission at the request of Judge J.H.S. Morison. In early March he made a trip to Teller to minister to the Catholics there, but was back in Nome for the Holy Week ceremonies and Easter, which were "very well attended."[5] During April he went to Pilgrim Hot Springs Mission north of Nome to give the children's retreat, his first — but, according to Edward J. Cunningham, S.J., Superior at the mission, "It was well received and the children enjoyed it very much."[6]

From Pilgrim Springs Cunningham went to Teller for ten days, where all of the Catholics and many non-Catholics came to all of the services and instructions. He also went to Wales, a village about 55 miles northwest of Teller, with a borrowed dog team, at the request of some Eskimo residents, and gave several well-attended instructions and baptized a baby.[7]

Cunningham's practical bent had been put to a test shortly after his arrival in Nome when he fixed up the inside of the parish house. He also repaired the old St. Joseph's hall at the request of several lodges, which, along with Cunningham, used it often for a variety of functions. When May brought with it warm weather and the house-leveling and roof-mending season in Nome, Cunningham took advantage of it to fix the leaky roof of his house-chapel, as well as to help a neighbor. Ann L. Walsh, Nomeite at the time, wrote: "One bright day as he [Cunningham] walked along, he noticed Almer 'Slim' Rydeen on the roof of his home repairing shingles. Fr. Tom stopped, climbed the ladder and, as he visited with Slim, assisted him with the repairs."[8]

According to Walsh, Cunningham was "a friend of everyone, regardless of race or creed. As he walked down the street, he would stop and talk [with anyone]. Through his friendly manner, Fr. Tom was especially endeared to a number of non-Catholics, and he was a great source of solace in time of serious illness and death." James M. Walsh, Ann's brother, recalled Cunningham's saying about himself that, when in Nome, he never missed a day visiting the hospital and the jail. Edmund A. Anable, S.J., who served with Cunningham in Nome, confirmed this.[9]

Cunningham's lifelong compassion for the downtrodden and the "underdog" was shown early in Nome when he did not hesitate to bury, "from the Church," an old-timer, Barney Kelly, who, "presumably of unsound mind," had allegedly committed suicide by drowning near Cape Nome.[10]

Cunningham regarded all of the Seward Peninsula as his parish, and covered a good part of it during his year in Nome. To a Jesuit friend he wrote, "My procedure was always the same, study of the various changes of dialect in each village, and teaching catechism to the children in the afternoon and to the adults at night. In between times, when I had the dishes washed, dogs fed, and the wood chopped against the next morning, I would do what I could towards easing the various bodily ailments to which the Eskimo is prone. I relied as often as not on the Grace of God as on my own medical knowledge. Anyhow, I produced some surprising results, and didn't kill anyone."[11]

Cunningham also wrote in the same letter about the more private side of a priest's life in Nome. When he received the letter from his friend, Cunningham said that his "spirit was low, I don't mean low in the wrong sense of the word, but that lowness that comes from a long, miserable, cold winter, with always a couple more months to go, and a lowness that is increased by bad grub, hard work, and loneliness.

"Much to my astonishment I was assigned on my return to Alaska to Nome. Nome has the reputation of wreaking havoc in the minds and bodies of the clergy. Of my predecessors one went completely mad, one froze to death, three lasted a year and then had to leave through ill health. I have been here since September, 1935, alone, and believe me, it's no picnic. I have been to confession once since then, when I went 50 miles out of my way to call on my neighbor in Kotzebue 200 miles north of here.

"When I saw what I was up against, I drew up a schedule to be followed as closely as possible here [in Nome] and when traveling. The day was divided from 5:00 a.m. to 10:30 p.m. between prayer, study, teaching catechism, and manual labour, in such a way that I didn't have time to sit down and feel sorry for myself."

Cunningham was an undoubted success as pastor of the Nome parish in the eyes of both his Superiors and parishioners. He befriended many in Nome, not only Catholics, but also Protestants and uncommitted, and was called "Father Tom" by all, even though it was not the custom at the time for Jesuits to be addressed or referred to by their first names. Joseph F. McElmeel, S.J., wrote to Bishop Crimont from Nulato on 30 April 1936, "that very good reports come from Nome about Father Tom Cunningham," and Lafortune, who knew well what kind of priest the Seward Peninsula area needed, urged Crimont to stop off in Ireland on his way to Rome to find "a Father like Fr. Th. Cunningham." James Walsh, one of his parishioners, echoed the sentiment of all Nome: "Fr. Tom seemed to fit right in with the people in Nome and the Eskimos.

He had great public relations; knew everyone in Nome — perhaps Seward Peninsula. He seemed to have been born for that work in that part of the world...a true missionary."[12]

Although Cunningham had expressed a "great desire to labor in the Kotzebue district," he was reassigned, to Little Diomede Island, toward the end of his Nome year. But he was not disappointed by his assignment, for he had written to Crimont, when Lafortune first suggested Cunningham's transfer, that he was "perfectly ready." Lafortune, who knew from personal experience what the Diomede assignment entailed, considered Cunningham particularly well suited for that station: "He has lots of pep, and lots of experience on the sea and with boats. Moreover, he begins to speak Eskimo, and that goes to the heart of the Natives more than anything else." Cunningham sailed on the *North Star*, the Bureau of Indian Affairs ship, for Little Diomede on 13 October 1936.[13]

4 / Little Diomede Island: 1936-1937

About 50 miles below the Arctic Circle, and exactly in the middle of Bering Strait — 57 miles of water that separate the two continents of North America and Asia — lie two immense crags of granite rock, Big Diomede and Little Diomede Islands, so named by Vitus Bering, who "discovered" the larger one in 1728 on the feast of St. Diomede, a Russian Orthodox saint. Separated by the international date line, Big Diomede now belongs to the Soviet Union, and Little Diomede to the United States. For countless generations the two islands, less than three miles apart, served as steppingstones between Siberia and Alaska, the Eskimos living on them acting as middlemen for the trade that flowed between the two continents; but since 1948, an invisible, but virtually impenetrable, iron curtain has hung between them.

Little Diomede Island is about two miles long and a bit over a mile wide. It rises abruptly out of the icy blue-green waters of Bering Strait to a plateau 1308 feet above sea level. The flanks of the island are almost perpendicular cliffs on all sides with the exception of the west side where a massive rock slide has created a more gentle slope, at the foot of which is the only boat landing place, a narrow beach of water-worn boulders 300 yards long. Even this is covered by breakers in stormy weather. The southwest slope is the only habitable corner of the island, where the village of Ignaluk has stood since prehistoric times.

The mainland Eskimos call the Diomeders the *imaangmiut*, "the people of the open water" — the open water being the ever-shifting leads in the ever-moving pack ice ("the ice that never sleeps") that chokes Bering Strait from October to July.[1] It is in this open water, in these leads, and on these ice fields that seals and migrating herds of walrus

This photo of the village of Igmaluk on Little Diomede Island appeared in *The National Geographic Magazine*, April 1951. St. Jude's Church, with attached priest's quarters, is perched upper right. *(Photo credit: Audrey and Frank Morgan)*

abound. From these marine mammals come the meat, skins, oil, and ivory so basic to the Diomede way of life. It is this readily available marine mammal resource that has kept the Diomeders on their seemingly inhospitable island up to the present day.

In addition to the riches of the sea, the island itself is a source of substantial quantities of food despite its apparent barrenness, for it has an abundance of low, matted plant life. Manure deposited over centuries by the countless birds that summer on the island has enriched the thin soil, enabling many species of plants, mosses, and lichens to flourish during the brief summer. The islanders gather the "Eskimo potato," an edible tuber, and greens, which are eaten fresh or preserved in seal oil or water to supplement seal and walrus meat during the winter. In summer birds and their eggs are also taken in great quantities.[2]

Cunningham was not the first missionary to go to Little Diomede, nor the first Catholic missionary to evangelize the Diomeders. Norwegian Lutherans had been on Little Diomede in the 1920s and 1930s, but had left, and Father Lafortune, as early as 1904, had sought out the Diomeders to bring them into the Catholic fold during their summer journeys to Nome to trade, to work for wages, and to carve and sell ivory. Then, in the summer of 1932, he joined the Diomeders on their island for the first time, established a temporary mission in an old house, and catechized and visited the people.[3] (To visit and be visited are among the basic joys of Eskimo life.)

Immediately upon his arrival on Little Diomede, Cunningham set about finishing the combination rectory and church building which the Diomeders had begun with lumber that Lafortune had sent them. During the two weeks of construction, he lived in the old house that had served as a temporary mission.[4]

On 5 November Cunningham began to keep a diary of the Little Diomede mission. From this we learn that it did not take him long to organize his activities into a more or less regular routine. There was Mass every weekday morning at 7:00 ("very well attended"); Sunday Mass was at 10:00 a.m. ("not so very well attended"). Every afternoon he held catechism classes for the children from 2:30 to 4:00. Instruction classes for adults were held on Wednesdays and Fridays at 6:00 p.m., and on Sundays at 7:00 p.m. From the outset he spoke Eskimo to the extent of his ability when teaching, instructing, preaching, or dealing with the people in general, and on 5 November, in his first diary entry, he wrote, "Preaching my first Eskimo sermon without help of interpreter this morning."

A.M.D.G.

St. Jude's Church. Iqualit. Little Diomede Island
Alaska.

In October 1936 the first priest to winter on Little
Diomede Island arrived with most of the Natives on the
North Star. Unloading began on Sunday Oct 16th and
for two or three days little else was done. Fr. Cunningham
lived in the old small house in the Village for the first two
weeks till the Church and living room were finished.

Quite a lot of work had to be done inside the Church, i.e.
build an altar, some kind of a sacristy, put wainscoting
on the wall etc. One stove burning Diesel Oil 27+ will be
used in the Church and a similar stove in the living room.
The oil burner will be installed in the Church when all the
rubbish has been burned.

There is mass every morning at 7 a.m. very well attended.
Catechism classes for the children every day from 2.30 till 4.
The adults have instruction on Wednesday Friday at 6 p.m. an
on Sunday at 7 p.m. Mass on Sunday is at 10 a.m. This is
not so very well attended so far (Nov. 5th). As yet the natives don't
seem to understand the obligation of Sunday mass. However with
the grace of God this will come in time Kakutai's son was
born the day of our arrival and was baptised the next day

First page of Father Tom's "Little Diomede Diary." This diary was begun on 5 November
1936. *(Oregon Province Archives)*

The Eskimos of Little Diomede spoke Inupiaq, which is the language of all Eskimos north of Unalakleet on Norton Sound, across all of northern Alaska and Canada, and in Greenland, and is quite similar to what Cunningham had studied in Nome. In spite of his linguistic ability, he had to struggle for some years before he became proficient in it.

Ever practical and resourceful, he devised a method for learning Eskimo that combined vocabulary building with seal hunting and cod fishing. When ice began to form around the island, he joined the men of the village on their seal hunts, and, along with his hunting gear, took with him a list of new Eskimo words and phrases and their meanings. He repeated these over and over to himself as he squatted by a lead waiting for a seal to surface, or knelt by a hole "jigging fish."[5]

In learning Eskimo Cunningham practiced himself what he preached to others. He felt very strongly that one should speak Eskimo when among Eskimos. He told Segundo Llorente, S.J., that, if he, Cunningham, were ever General Superior of the Jesuits in Alaska, he would force the priests coming to Alaska to learn the language first, even if it should take them ten years to do so. "He was adamant on this."[6]

Diet on Little Diomede may have been of concern to most white men, but not to Cunningham. He wrote to his brother John that "the food problem is not acute. If I have two sacks of flour, one of sugar, and twelve pounds of tea per year, I have all I need. Except for bread and tea, I live on the same grub as the Natives: seal meat, walrus meat, polar bear steak — when lucky enough to come across any — various kinds of fish that the Arctic provides." Bread, which he baked, he allowed himself "as a consideration for my gentle upbringing on a backwoods farm."[7]

Since guns and hunting had been a big part of Cunningham's life from boyhood, it did not take him long to establish himself on Little Diomede as an able hunter. "The Natives respect me as a hunter," he wrote during his second winter on the island, and, indeed, one Diomeder described him as "a pretty good shot."[8] While on Diomede, Cunningham regularly took one day a week off to hunt for himself and to help out several families who had no hunters. To keep himself in meat, oil, and skins for clothes, he needed an average of two seals per week. But he did not always get his two seals on his weekly hunt day. "Sometimes I don't even get one," he wrote to his brother. "I have sat on an ice cake freezing to death for as much as four hours at a time without even seeing one. And there is nothing more maddening than sitting on a cake of ice for three hours and then missing the only seal that comes up. I wonder there are no swear words in the Eskimo language."

He went on to describe seal hunting to his brother: "To get them you have to go out to the moving ice, often five miles away from the solid ice around the island. When you come to the moving ice, you pick out a good spot and watch for a seal to come up in the open water between the floating cakes and let him have a bullet between the eyes. You have to be pretty quick and a reasonably good shot, as the seal takes only about half a minute to breathe, and he presents not more than a six-inch target. Occasionally on the big ice fields there are breathing holes made by seals themselves, and if one has a harpoon ready, he can easily hook them."

The population of Little Diomede numbered about 140 in 1936. Half were Catholics, some were Lutherans, and some, mostly recent arrivals from Big Diomede, were non-Christians, whose conversion he considered an important part of his ministry. He welcomed Lutherans into the Catholic fold, but did not pursue them very aggressively. He was fairly successful in making converts, since he regularly recorded baptisms of adults in the church diary. Still, he was slow to baptize anyone whose sincerity or preparedness he doubted.

He did not limit his convert-making zeal to Little Diomede, for from the time he arrived, he looked across to Big Diomede and the Siberian mainland with a view to proselytizing there as well. During the 1930s, there was still a fair amount of contact between the Eskimos of the two Diomedes and the Siberian coast, and just one month after his arrival, Cunningham joined the Little Diomede men on a trading trip to Big Diomede because he needed some cloth to make a curtain to hang in front of the altar he had recently built for his new church. "It seems ironical," he noted in the diary, "buying cloth in a Soviet store for decoration inside a Catholic Church."

When Big Diomeders came to Little Diomede, they always visited Cunningham and were "very friendly and sociable. The schoolteacher especially is very sociable."[9] He made his first contact with Siberians through the Big Diomeders. In January, 1937, according to the diary, "Some Siberians wintering on Big Diomede came here. All visited me and I took the opportunity to instruct them a little. They are warned against anything having to do with religion." In March he was again "over to Big Diomede and even instructed the people a little bit."

Late in April the men of Diomede harpooned and landed a whale, which for the hunters was a source of great pride, and for the whole village cause for joy and celebration. But Cunningham was neither impressed nor elated by their feat, and described the kill as "more or less suicide on the whale's part." He looked upon it as a mixed blessing. The meat and blubber were very welcome, of course, but "the catching of the whale revived many superstitions even among the Catholics." He persuaded the Catholic men to "promise as far as they could to try and kill these superstitions and themselves to have no part in them."[10] The special dances to appease the soul of the whale were to take place the following autumn.

On the general subject of superstition, Cunningham wrote, "The chief difficulties in the way of conversion were superstitions, and a certain laxity in the moral laws of marriage."[11] Evidently two wholly diverse cultures, the Eskimo and the Christian, were here in conflict. Cunningham's judgments regarding superstitions were, predictably, ethnocentric. To the Diomeders of the time, the term "superstitions," as in the above context, was meaningless. They had little difficulty reconciling their traditional whaling ceremonialism — their shamanistic rites, cleansing rituals, traditional whaling songs for success of the hunt, use of charms and amulets, their taboos, their celebrations of a successful hunt — with their relatively new Christian faith with its priest, its Mass, its penitential rite, its hymns, its prayers for daily bread, its prayers of thanksgiving, its medals and statues of Christ and the saints. Viewing life pragmatically, they saw little essential difference between the traditional and the new.

Unlike many early-day missionaries in Alaska, Cunningham did not object to the traditional Eskimo dances. In fact, he himself could often be seen sitting among the men in the "orchestra" beating a drum. Sometimes, when the villagers had entertained him with their dances, they insisted that he reciprocate in some similar way, so — to their genuine amusement — he would put a record on the phonograph and dance an Irish jig.[12]

On 27 May 1937 Cunningham returned to Nome from Little Diomede "hale and hearty," according to Lafortune. All things considered, his first year on Diomede was a successful one. He survived the year well physically — despite inadequate living quarters — and his spiritual ministry was so fruitful that Bishop Crimont wrote in his 1937 report to Rome: "Rev. Thomas Cunningham, although only 31 years old and the youngest among the missionaries of northern Alaska, has, nevertheless, undertaken, ably and generously, the difficult labor of preaching the gospel among the Eskimos of Diomede Island, and through his dedication has made them such good Christians that it will be hard for him to desert them."

But during that summer away from the island, Cunningham was less concerned about the impression he was making in Rome than about the *Harvey E*, a boat he had bought and had shipped from Seattle to Nome so as to be "independent of the odd freighter or government boat that does service to my island."[13]

Unfortunately, the *Harvey E*, which arrived in Nome on 23 June, never did live up to expectations. Her engine was old and needed "a good deal of coaxing" before it would start. However, after making a short trial run, Cunningham was "more than pleased" with her, and on 1 July he and a few King Islanders set out for Sledge Island to gather eggs. It turned out to be an ill-fated trip. The engine gave trouble, and one of the flanges of the propeller shaft broke. To add to their misery, the sea was so rough that — for the first time in his life — Cunningham became seasick. They had to be towed back to Nome.[14] The *Harvey E* continued to give much trouble that summer and thereafter, but Cunningham did not give up on her until she had given him several years of reluctant service.

While in Nome in the summer of 1937 — in fact, whenever he was in Nome — Cunningham never lacked for dinner invitations. When invited, he would ask what was on the menu. If it was to his liking, he would accept the invitation; if not, he would say, "I'll take a rain check."

When he felt like eating out, but had no invitation, he would simply invite himself to someone's home. "Hello, Betty! What's for supper?" he would ask a friend on the phone. "Leg-o-lamb, with mint." "I'll be right over." "Lamb" meant both "New Zealand" and "Ireland," and that appealed to Cunningham. "No one felt slighted by his manner."[15] Segundo Llorente, who was with him in Nome for a time, wrote, "He would call people before supper and ask them to add an extra potato, because he would soon be coming for dinner. And, amazingly, people just loved it coming from him. He was famous all around as nice company."[16]

"I met Father Cunningham only once," wrote another of his Nome acquaintances, "when he came, unexpectedly, to visit me at our very frontier-like, unpainted house at Nome one afternoon...He certainly was a gaunt, skinny young man when he appeared, but he had such a roguish Irish twinkle in his eye and was a real tease. I, being young and flustered at receiving a guest so unexpectedly — especially a priest — apologized profusely for the 'untidy' look of my small, very dusty cabin-home. My apologies were met with an unsympathetic, 'Oh, come off it! You know very well you haven't bothered dusting this place for a month!' He was a real rough kidder...He was much loved by the people of Nome...His dropping in unexpectedly was taken in stride by all."[17]

After a good holiday on the mainland, to which most of his Little Diomede parishioners also went during the summer, Cunningham left Nome on the *North Star* at midnight, 24 October, for his second winter on the island.[18]

5 / Little Diomede Island: 1937-1939

Foul weather and storms out of the south hit Little Diomede in early November, 1937. One storm was so severe that it endangered the first row of houses on the beach. "None of the old Natives could remember a storm quite as bad," wrote Cunningham in the Diomede diary. It took him and the villagers three weeks to move supplies, that had been unloaded a half mile southwest, to the village.[1]

In mid-November he began to add to his living quarters, which Ménager, who had visited Diomede on 9 May, described as "about the poorest I have ever seen anywhere. They are of the two by four variety, and by sitting in the center of his room he can almost reach every corner."[2] The new addition was finished by the end of November; but, though the remodeled living quarters gave him more space, they were "awful cold" because of insufficient insulating materials, and a winter colder than usual. On 28 March 1938 he wrote to Father Paul O'Connor, "Believe it or not, it was 15 degrees below zero inside the house when I got up this morning. I cannot afford to have a fire going all night."

Cunningham had to economize on fuel because he had an annual budget of only $250, and, furthermore, had lost half of his coal and some of his oil supply in that severe November storm.[3] By the following winter, his house was much warmer, due to the intervention of McElmeel, General Superior of the Alaska Mission, who took pity on him and borrowed enough money for proper insulation. McElmeel wrote to Crimont, "We must see to it that Father is given decent quarters and a sufficient supply of food. More than that he WILL [sic] not accept."[4]

But he did have electricity, even on remote Little Diomede Island! His living quarters were lighted by one bulb drawing power from a small electric light plant. The Eskimo name for the light was "the lamp that makes you numb...After a few mild shocks the people understand the idea."[5]

Cunningham's round of activities during his second winter on Little Diomede was similar to that of his first winter. From time to time he visited the Eskimos on Big Diomede. "I go over there on the ice occasionally," he once wrote, "and have already given instruction to those Natives. The Soviet Gov't sent word that I was not supposed to visit their island. But the Natives won't tell on me; and, besides, there are already four Catholics there."[6]

A confrontation between Cunningham and Soviet officials was not long in coming, however. When he again ventured over to Big Diomede in June, he knew full well that "they [the Soviets] don't seem to like priests,"[7] and he has left an account of what happened in letters to Jesuit seminarian "Mr." Buchanan, written on 14 November 1938, and to O'Connor. To Buchanan he wrote:

"Last summer, June 22nd to be exact, I was arrested over there by some Soviet officers (whites) who happened to be making an official visit to the island. They had a gun on me before I could even think of my own revolver, and they held me to take me to the mainland. The Eskimos who were in the boat with me immediately armed themselves with rifles and harpoons and surrounded the house where I was held, and threatened to shoot every Russian in sight unless I were released immediately. At what I thought was a good moment, I made a dive for a Russian, gun and all, and got out the door. The Eskimos then surrounded me, and we all kept the officers in their own jail till we were ready to go. It was quite exciting, for a while, but I admit I was scared."

To O'Connor: "The Soviets caught me while hunting walrus last June. We were pushed up by the ice on a Soviet island, and I [was] no sooner on the rocks before an officer, done up in buttons and revolver, arrested me. It was only by saying that the Natives would shoot him that I persuaded him that it would be healthier to let me go. The authorities held me for three hours. The latest report is that there are 1000 roubles on my head."[8]

Lafortune, referring to Cunningham's altercation with the Russians, wrote to Crimont's secretary, William G. Levasseur, S. J., on 4 July 1938, "He had an encounter with the Soviets. The thing might have had dire effects if the Russians had dared to put their hands on him. The

Natives were fidgeting with their guns and the Father himself had a revolver hidden under his parky [Eskimo coat], ready for action." This was apparently Cunningham's last trip to Big Diomede.

On 26 June, just four days after he had his run-in with the Soviets, Cunningham arrived in Nome. The Nome diarist noted that he looked "a little thin." A week later, McElmeel arrived in Nome for his official visitation, and on 10 July he wrote to Bishop Crimont, "Fathers Lafortune and Tom Cunningham are here from their rival islands. What splendid missionaries they truly are. Their work engrosses them there and here." McElmeel went on to mention that Cunningham was "very thin"; also that he heard him preach in Eskimo, and that Lafortune told him that Cunningham's preaching was "very good." Twelve days later, McElmeel again wrote Crimont that "Father Tom Cunningham is heart and soul in his work on Little Diomede."

On 6 August Cunningham and Lafortune renovated the Nome house-chapel. Later that month Cunningham rounded up his Diomeders for examinations by a doctor from Juneau. During his years with the Diomeders, he was constantly concerned about their health and general welfare, and was frequently called upon to play the role of doctor on the island.

As in most pioneer missionary situations, confrontations between the missionary and the "medicine man," the *angatkuq* or shaman, were a common occurrence. During the first quarter of this century, the Lutheran missionaries on Diomede and Lafortune in Nome fought it out with the shamans.[9] By the time Cunningham arrived on the island, shamanism was on the decline, but by no means dead. It was not long before he and the shaman met head on, not only in matters of religion, but also of medicine, with a vigor that prompted Fr. Lafortune to say that Cunningham "has lots of grit and gives the remnants of the medicine men a mighty tough time."[10]

Cunningham gave a graphic account of his dealings with the Little Diomede shaman in an address to the Women's Sodality of Elmendorf Air Force Base:

"Now when I went to Diomede Island, it was a constant battle between myself and the shaman, whose name was Izaqaziiq. And Izaqaziiq: he probably was a good man — although he showed no great evidence of sanctity when I knew him. Oh, he liked me, and when I started giving instructions, his wife and the three children used to come. I was kind of hesitant about baptizing them, you know. He had a great hand at playing tricks, like all the shamans, and he'd play all sorts of tricks when he felt his power going down a little. There were some that were rather astounding.

"One victory I had over him concerned an Eskimo by the name of Imaneinna. He was an old Eskimo, probably in his sixties. He didn't do very much except go out and fish through the ice. And when he was walking home, he slipped on some glare ice and broke his arm. When he came home, his wife came up and asked me if I would go down and fix up his arm, and I did.

"Well, the bone — it was a nice, clean break, above the elbow — and no trouble at all setting it. And then I made a splint, a right angle, out of plywood, and I bound his arm to this plywood splint, and I said, 'Now you leave it that way. And I'll come down every day or so, and see how it is getting along.' And he said, 'Yes, Father.'

"And then the next day I'd go down, and it was obvious that the splint had been taken off, and they tried to put it back the same way. And I asked them, 'How come?' — and figured out the medicine man had been down and convinced old Imaneinna that the reason why he broke his arm was that he had not been offering sacrifice to the souls of the fish he was getting, and the fish were upset about it. So, I bound up his arm again and asked him, 'Now, you just leave that be!' And I said, 'If you're going to be pulling that off all the time, you might just as well not bother.'

"Well, the next time I go down, it was obvious that the thing had been taken off again. So I said, 'Now listen! There's no such thing as professional jealousy here, or religious jealousy at all.' I said, 'If you want to do it the medicine man's way, that's fine too.' I says, 'It's perfectly all right with me, but it's one or the other.'

"And so I let it go three or four days, and then it obviously happened again. So I went out through the little tunnel entrance of the house, and I picked up a chunk of the rib of a whale about the size of a baseball bat, and I brought that in. And he said, 'What are you going to do with that?' And I said, 'I'm going to break your arm all over again, and let the medicine man take care of it, because, obviously, you want him to do it instead of me, and he has to start from scratch, so I'm going to leave your arm the way I found it.' And he didn't like that, and then he asked me to change my mind. And his wife begged me. Of course, I had no intention of doing it, but he didn't know that.

"'Well,' I said, 'send over for the medicine man, and I will explain things to him.' So they did, and he came in. And I said, 'Now, Izaqaziiq, this is not a question of professional jealousy at all. He asked me to take care of his arm, and I've been doing it, but you've been interfering and going through your routine, so I give up and I turn it all over to you, but you're not going to have an unfair advantage. You start from scratch.' And, of course, he didn't want me to do it either.

"So, I laid down the rule that he could come and visit the way you visit a sick person, but no more medicine, and no more religion being mixed into it. And he said, 'Yes, Father.' And, anyway, eventually the arm got all right, and Izaqaziiq used to come around, and he wanted instructions.

"So, I figured that if an Eskimo of the ordinary run of the mill needed one year, old Izaqaziiq would need about five. Anyway, he got baptized after two years." On 29 November 1936 Cunningham wrote in the Little Diomede diary that he baptized Izaqaziiq's three daughters, and that Izaqaziiq himself and his wife were asking for baptism. "We will see," was Cunningham's reaction at the time.

It would be wrong to infer from the above that Cunningham shared the common cliché that Eskimos were a simple, naive, childlike people, for he also observed in his talk to the Women's Sodality that "an Eskimo is not a fool by any means; [they are] very, very shrewd people, and they are very, very intelligent."

In 1938 Cunningham's Nome summer came to an end on 20 September when he, in his own boat, the *Harvey E*, left for Little Diomede, where a severe winter and occasional food and fuel shortages awaited him and the Diomeders.[11]

The early fall hunting was good. "Quite a few walrus and one polar bear have been caught to date," he wrote in the diary on 6 November. "There is now lots of fresh meat, a godsend, and plenty of oil." Ten days later he recorded, "The ice is continually moving in and out. The weather is very cold. North wind all the time and already nearly three feet of snow."

December brought with it "very cold weather. An extra strong south wind broke up the ice and pushed water and ice over 100 feet up the island. We had to work very hard to save the oil and coal. Fortunately, very little was lost. Walrus are being killed the odd time. Meat and blubber, however, are scarce." 15 December: "The cold weather continues." 15 January 1939: "Weather extremely cold. Very high wind and $-30°$ every day so far. Hunting impossible, and wind and cold. Food and oil scarce." 30 January: "Extreme cold keeps up. It's very hard to have the house warm enough to be comfortable. No hunting. I have had to give away several sacks of coal and nearly all the canned meat. It leaves me short, but I cannot see the people cold and starving. The Gov't [schoolteacher] doesn't seem to worry." 5 February: "The weather let up for two days and we had good hunting. South wind and current. But it lasted only two days. Now it's cold as ever." 12 February: "Everything still frozen up. No hunting, but the men fish for a while everyday and are fairly lucky." March: "No change. Weather always exceptionally cold. Coal all gone. Use old lumber for cooking. The majority of the people suffering a lot from cold and hunger. The Gov't does nothing to help." 1 April: "North wind suddenly stopped today and south wind with strong blizzard started up. The temperature, however, rose considerably."

On 13 April Cunningham wrote to Levasseur, "We are getting near the end of what is probably the worst winter the island has known. The old men tell me they have never experienced anything like it, and when one considers that these old men, like all old men, are inclined to exaggerate the discomforts of previous generations, the statement can be considered the truth. It's true we have never been so near dying from cold and hunger. It was just too cold to hunt and, of course, that meant no seals, and no seals means no oil to heat the homes, and no meat in the pot...We have been on very short rations since three months, one meal a day, in fact."

By mid-April things took a turn for the better. On the 15th Cunningham wrote in the diary, "Fairly good hunting. Worst of trouble is over. Nearly everyone has meat and oil."

Wien pilot Jack Hermann landed on the ice at Diomede on 13 May, and Cunningham flew to Nome with him that same day to arrange to have supplies sent to the island store. Father Llorente, pastor of Kotzebue, in Nome for the summer, wrote in the Nome diary that "Fr. Tom Cunningham arrived from Diomede [in the evening]. Fr. Tom came to get a load of food and ammunition; looks thin, or rather, emaciated, the eyes sunk and ever shivering. He admits that he has suffered true, real and unadulterated hunger this winter. Being practically penniless, I loaned him $50 to be paid back within the next 99 years."

Three days later Llorente wrote, "Fr. Tom gets a royal welcome from the Nome folks, and a few substantial donations for his islanders." The following day, 17 May, Cunningham returned to the island with a planeload of food, ammunition, and other essentials, and a Wien Alaska Airlines plane made four more trips with supplies.

Throughout his life it was characteristic of Cunningham to help those in need — whether real or only apparent — no matter at what cost to himself, or, at times, to others. Llorente, who knew him well, wrote that Cunningham "had absolutely no sense of money. He would give everything to anybody. I had bought salmon strips in the store, expensive food indeed, and I had hoped to enjoy them for days to come. Just then he came to the kitchen and ate one strip. A Native man came to visit him. Tom took the whole bundle of strips and gave it to him to take home. He would give away a radio, a camera, anything and everything. So, he was perennially broke. When he was alone in Nome, if he had money left, he would not take up the Sunday collection. People soon learned that when the collection was taken, Father had spent his last cent and needed the money."[12]

Cunningham was compassionate and generous to a fault. But, by the same token, whenever he was in need — real or apparent — people came quickly and generously to his aid. It was, however, not only his overt, tangible compassion and prodigality that moved people to reciprocate in kind. There was also something about the man himself, something about his quiet, soft-spoken wistful manner that never failed to elicit sympathy toward him and a readiness to help.

6 / Mont-Laurier, Quebec: 1939-1940

As a general rule, in the 1930s, Jesuits made what they call "Tertian-ship" shortly after finishing theological studies. A Tertianship was then a ten-month period — following the many years of academic studies — during which the young Jesuit was meant to renew himself spiritually. He devoted long hours to prayer and meditation. He studied the Constitutions and the spirit of the Society of Jesus, and reflected on the implications of his living the rest of his life in it.

By 1939 Cunningham was overdue for Tertianship, and the question of his making it had already been raised by Superiors for several years. He himself wrote on 20 October 1938 to a friend, "Next year possibly I will return for Tertianship. A little polishing up won't do any harm."[1] Nevertheless, the following summer, he pleaded with Alaska Mission Superior McElmeel to be allowed to spend another year on Little Diomede, to further consolidate his gains there. Several reasons, however, compelled McElmeel to send him out for Tertianship. "First of all," he wrote on 20 June 1939 to Crimont's recently consecrated coadjutor, Bishop Walter J. Fitzgerald, S.J., "his health is just about shattered by the awful experiences of this past year. Then, too, he will have to learn quite definitely to follow strict orders about his manner of living on the island. He tries to support all the Eskimos...A year of quiet thinking would enable our devoted Father Tom to see how best to order his life on the island."

Cunningham left Nome for Tertianship at Mont-Laurier, Quebec, on 27 July. On his way to Canada, he stopped off in Seattle. While there, he offered Mass early one morning in a certain convent. The Sisters noticed nothing unusual about the visiting priest other than that he was young, rather thin, with a definitely weather-beaten face and a distinctive accent to his Latin. It was only when he began to say the prayers at the end of Mass that it became evident to them that the visitor was someone out of the ordinary — for the language he used resembled nothing any of them had ever heard before. It was, in fact, the most astonishing lingual explosion that had ever been heard in that convent. The language was, of course — Little Diomede Eskimo.

Wonderment grew when, during breakfast, the mystery priest asked the Sister serving him if she knew who had won the Spanish civil war and who the new pope was. About himself he said only that he was a foreigner.[2] Cunningham knew very well, of course, who had won the war and who the new pope was; but, from his winters on remote Diomede, where news was indeed scarce and late in coming, he got the idea for this captivating and plausible act. In the convent he had the perfect setting for putting it on.[3]

This was wholly in keeping with his character. He had a great sense of humor — the subtle, teasing kind — and a good feel for audiences. He was an accomplished *raconteur;* indeed, according to Llorente, "He had the gift of the gab, a talent to monopolize the conversation with tales

The Jesuit Tertianship at Mont-Laurier, the south side, August 1938, before landscaping.
(Archives de la Compagnie de Jésus, Province du Canada-français)

that kept listeners gasping. He spoke [slowly], always in a low voice
to force listeners to listen if they did not want to miss what he was
saying," a technique that gave him an aura of remoteness bordering
on mystery.[4]

Little is known about Cunningham's stay at Mont-Laurier, except that
he was hospitalized once for an unspecified operation, but he emerged,
"a perfect physical specimen," according to his doctor.[5]

While Cunningham was enjoying — or, at least, surviving — the
solitude of that "year of quiet thinking" at Mont-Laurier, McElmeel
was devoting much thought and letter-writing to his case. He wrote
to Bishop Fitzgerald on 11 January 1940 that "His Paternity [Wlodimir
Ledochowski in Rome, the Father General of all the Jesuits] writes me
that it is his opinion that Little Diomede is too circumscribed a field
for a missionary of [Cunningham's] ability." McElmeel felt that Cunningham, in his desire to be all things to all men, was going too far,
and that, therefore, "if he returns to Little Diomede, his hunting must
be strictly prohibited??[sic], or, at least, very much moderated."

McElmeel further suggested to Fitzgerald that Cunningham should
be reassigned, to Nelson Island, on his return to Alaska, but he overlook-
ed — or chose to ignore — the very serious consideration that the Nelson
Island language, Central Yup'ik, is a language quite different from that
of Diomede, which Cunningham had learned at great cost of time and
effort. McElmeel, however, had his reasons for proposing that Cunningham be reassigned. "Nome is not a good place for Father Tom. In
fact, such restrictions will have to be placed on him when he returns
that he will find it extremely hard to knuckle down. Father Tom's period
of dare-devil exploits is now at an end, and he must settle down to
constructive missionary work."

It seems that McElmeel's views concerning Cunningham had become
somewhat distorted by the latter's rather singular lifestyle, for from
McElmeel's own prior testimony it is evident that Cunningham was indeed doing "constructive missionary work." Witness, too, the all-out effort Cunningham had made to master the Native language, to catechize,
to instruct, and to convert the Diomeders.

In several follow-up letters to Fitzgerald, McElmeel spells out further
what concerned him regarding Cunningham. On 13 February 1940 he
wrote from Nome, "It will soon be necessary to determine the status
of Father Tom Cunningham for the coming year...First of all, he is
very well liked here. He has many friends among non-Catholics, is popular

with them, but does not seem to influence them in matters of religion.
He is admired for his living on Little Diomede under exceedingly difficult
circumstances. However, we have to look to the future and weigh every
possible reason for keeping him on the island or moving him to some
other place."

What seems to have concerned McElmeel about Cunningham, above
all, was "his drinking. No one has ever seen him under the influence
of liquor, but it is well known that he drinks much more than he should
if he wants to have influence in preventing the Eskimos from doing
the same." Empty bottles in the Nome rectory attic, as well as the word
of Lafortune, supported McElmeel's claim that Cunningham did unquestionably do more than merely "drown the shamrock on St. Pat's Day
with a little nip of whiskey."

It is no secret that throughout his priestly years Cunningham drank
often, and at times heavily. Still, he never saw his drinking as a serious
personal problem,[6] and vehemently defended his right to drink when
confronted by Superiors. For the most part he seems to have been quite
successful in keeping his use of alcohol from hampering his priestly work,
and to the extent that people knew about it, they were not offended.
Even McElmeel wrote to Fitzgerald, "I must say that the people of
Nome do not seem to mind it that he likes his liquor." In fact, they
were the very ones who supplied most of it.

In 1940, Superiors were seriously contemplating sending Cunningham
to New Zealand to raise money to build a new mission boarding school
somewhere on the Seward Peninsula.[7] Remarks in various letters leave
no doubt that the idea for such a trip came from Cunningham himself,
for it had been 16 years since he had seen his family, and he longed
very much to see them again. However, before he could satisfy this
most natural of human longings, he had to wait a few more years.

Early in March 1940, Cunningham knew that he would be going
back to Little Diomede, notwithstanding the fact that Ledochowski in
Rome, Alaska Mission Superior McElmeel, and Coadjutor Bishop Fitzgerald all seriously questioned the advisability of his returning. Who,
then, was responsible for his reassignment to Diomede? The decision
was made by Bishop Crimont, who had the final say in such matters.
Crimont, writing to Oregon Province Provincial William G. Elliott, S.J.,
acknowledged that Cunningham had "too small a field of work at Diomede
for a man of youth and vigor," but he was persuaded that the results
Cunningham had already achieved on the island were such that he should

be reassigned to it. Numbers alone were not the determining factor in Crimont's eyes; it was quality results that counted. He wanted the Diomeders to have a solid foundation in their new faith before being deprived of a resident pastor.[8]

Cunningham's reaction to word that he would soon be back at his old station were predictable. To Elliott he wrote on 13 March, "I am going back to Diomede, which pleases me very much. I don't know exactly why, but I like that island, and I hope I am left there at least till all are Catholic, and the plant in general has the prosperous appearance of King Island." (Fr. Lafortune had established a mission on King Island in 1929.)

At the end of June, after Cunningham had left Mont-Laurier, the Father Rector of the Tertianship, Samuel Lemay, S.J., filled out the official report of Cunningham's ten months there. Lemay wrote that he made the thirty-day retreat "with edification and fidelity," that he performed humble duties "with diligence and a supernatural spirit," and that in his behavior he kept the rules faithfully and was noted for his fraternal charity and alacrity. He reported also that Cunningham was "gifted with the spiritual as well as with the temporal qualities that befit a good missionary."

7 / Little Diomede Island: 1940-1944

"My health is very good," Cunningham wrote to Crimont from Nome on 19 June 1940, "and, of course, the spirituality received quite an uplift in Tertianship," but on 11 August he wrote that he had "recently spent six days in the local hospital. Had a touch of the flu. After two days there I was in fine condition, and have never felt better than right now. The medical man says I am as sound as a brass bell — heart and lungs perfect, and not a nerve in my body."

Cunningham's letters are punctuated with almost monotonous regularity by comments on the excellence of his health, made, one suspects, because he was accused from time to time of neglecting it, and because he feared that the matter of his health might be used to keep him from Little Diomede. But, as a matter of fact, his health was not really all that good, and his frequent and exaggerated remarks about his soundness tended rather to disprove than to prove it. He protested too much.

Before "going home," as he put it, to Diomede on the *North Star*, Cunningham submitted his expense account for the year 1940-41 to Alaska Mission Superior McElmeel: "Groceries: $117.35, Hardware: $48.00, Coal: $53.00, Fuel: $160.00." McElmeel could only admire Cunningham for going off to the island for ten months with such a scanty amount of food, remarking that "Father Tom is one of the heroic figures in modern Alaska missionary life."[1]

Cunningham, "sound as a brass bell" in August, came down with a severe attack of quinsy in November. It was too late in the year to take him to Nome, or to bring medical aid from the mainland, so the schoolteachers, Mr. and Mrs. Norman Whitaker, took him into their quarters and nursed him back to health with instructions received via their radio from the doctor on the cutter *Haida* at Dutch Harbor and the doctor in Nome.[2] On 1 December he wrote in the Diomede diary that he was "able to resume [his] usual duties...The schoolteachers cannot be thanked too much," and on 8 January 1941, true to form, he wrote

Father Tom returning to Little Diomede in 1940. *(Oregon Province Archives)*

The notation on the back of this photo, taken circa 1940, reads: "This picture tells a story. Some years ago Fr. Tom and this Eskimo boy [Moses Milligrock] made the trip from Diomede to Nome in this small skinboat. Everyone was amazed when they landed safely in Nome." The notation is signed, "Jos. McElmeel." Father McElmeel was General Superior of the Jesuits in Alaska at the time. *(Oregon Province Archives)*

to Crimont, "Right now I feel in perfect health. . . The day is well filled with catechism, study of language, visiting sick, and, worst of all, the ordinary household chores." He finally had his tonsils removed that July in Nome, where he spent most of the summer ministering to the islanders who had come there to work and sell their ivory carvings.[3]

While Cunningham was in Nome, Bishop Fitzgerald arrived to confer with him and the Nome pastor, Joseph I. McHugh, S.J., about how the pastoral needs of the white community of Nome and those of the Eskimos of Nome and the outlying villages might best be met. It was decided that McHugh would continue on as pastor of the whites, and Eskimo-speaker Cunningham would be his assistant with full charge of the Natives in Nome and in the Seward Peninsula area. On 26 July Fitzgerald wrote to Crimont, "I was edified by the complete accord with which both Fathers received my directions, and Father Tom's humble acceptance of second place in the scheme excited my admiration. . . Father Tom is a wonderful missionary, and he will accomplish a lot of good for the Eskimos. He has great zeal for souls."

The first day of October, 1941, was a momentous one for Cunningham, for on that day in Nome, at the age of 35, he became a "Yank," a naturalized U.S. citizen. The Certificate of Naturalization gives his height as five feet ten inches, his weight as 148 pounds, and "complexion ruddy, color of eyes hazel, color of hair dark brown." Toward the end of his life, after he had made a name for himself as an arctic ice expert, the press — for poetic reasons, no doubt — ascribed to him "arctic blue eyes," but his driver's license, official military papers, and his own letters give the color as hazel.[4]

About 8 October Cunningham left Nome on the U.S. revenue cutter *Hermes* for his fifth winter on Diomede, where, on the 18th, his former patient, Imaneinna, died. "He was a tough old pagan," Cunningham wrote in the diary, "but he asked for baptism before his death." In a letter published in *Jesuit Missions*, Cunningham wrote, "I received [Imaneinna] into the Church the day before he died. He had never attended church all the time I knew him, but had learned the catechism from his son-in-law and daughter. Some kind of pagan pride had hindered him from openly expressing his belief. Before he died he gave his family and relatives a nice lecture on their duties towards the Church. He was a fine old character and I miss him."[5]

World War II erupted in the Pacific on 7 December 1941. Did news of that portentous, global event reach Little Diomede? We do not know.

Cunningham did not mention it in the Diomede diary. Always optimistic, never one to complain, he laconically summarized that historic month and year: "Quiet month...No complaints to make about anything. Good year all around."

From Diomede, on 26 January 1942, he wrote a rather lengthy letter to Elliott in which he referred, very much in passing, to "a couple of extra-curricular jobs" imposed on him by the Intelligence Department of the Army. Not surprisingly, little is known about what kind of intelligence work he was actually involved in during the summer of 1941 and later, during the war. There is ample evidence, however, that he was involved in such work: for example, he wrote in his official military record that he "worked with Army Intelligence intermittently for one year." Very likely he was asked to keep an eye out for possible Japanese activity in the Bering Strait area and to provide weather data.

Until 1942 he did not have a radio on the island, though he had possessed a radio operator's license for some years.[6] Under date of 31 August 1942, the Alaska Defense Command, Office of the Assistant Chief of Staff for Military Intelligence, informed "To whom it may concern," that it had "issued to Father THOMAS PATRICK CUNNINGHAM a 100-watt radio transmitter which is in his possession. It is contemplated that information of military interest will be transmitted by Father CUNN-INGHAM via Nome to the office interested from Little Diomede Island." All military authorities were requested to offer him cooperation and furnish him with "certain codes so that he can transmit meteorological data."

Father Edmund Anable also had proof of his activities: "One day in Nome, around 1944, three sharply dressed young men came to the rectory and asked for Father Tom. I told them he was away, out of town. We chatted a bit; then they opened their wallets and showed me cards identifying them as Navy intelligence men. They went on to tell me that all the information ever supplied by Father Tom proved to be absolutely exact and correct."[7]

In the late 1940s, Cunningham was an auxiliary chaplain in the Army Reserves with the rank of captain. Edward J. Fortier, himself an Army intelligence agent in Alaska during World War II, guessed that Cunningham was "the Army's best conduit for information on eastern Siberia." Fortier saw him land once at Elmendorf Air Force Base in those years with two generals on hand to meet him. "Obviously," concluded Fortier, "he was no ordinary reserve captain. I suspected, although I couldn't prove it, that when the Iron Curtain came down, Father Tom still had some kind of contacts among the Siberian Eskimos."[8]

During the winter of 1941-42, Cunningham was on Diomede only part of the time. Ace bush pilot Sigurd Wien landed at the island on 3 March, and several days later Cunningham flew with him to Nome, where, on the 14th, he "took his last vows"; that is, he pronounced for the last time the three vows of perpetual poverty, chastity, and obedience. In doing so, he became a "formed Jesuit," and he and the Society of Jesus became bound one to the other inseparably and forever.

To implement the "scheme" drawn up the previous July by Fitzgerald — according to which Cunningham, as McHugh's assistant, was to be "in complete charge of the Native work at Nome, Diomede Island, Teller, Pilgrim Springs, and [Marys] Igloo" — Cunningham, shortly after mid-March, headed north with his recently purchased dog team to minister to the Natives at Pilgrim Springs, Marys Igloo, and Teller.[9]

Given the new approach to taking care of Catholic pastoral needs in the Seward Peninsula area mentioned above, Cunningham could henceforth no longer regard Diomede as his one main concern. By this time most of the Diomeders were Catholic and well grounded in the faith. He saw the wisdom of Fitzgerald's decisions and accepted them graciously. He did, however, have one modest request. "For a sentimental reason," Fitzgerald wrote to Crimont, "[Cunningham] desires that the place where he has worked valiantly (Diomede) will not be erased from the *catalogus*." Cunningham's desire was granted, and his name and that of Little Diomede continued to be linked in the Oregon Province Catalog.[10]

Cunningham — helped by a man and a boy — spent much of the summer and fall of 1942 at the Pilgrim Springs mission putting in and tending a garden. This combination mission and orphanage had been closed the year before because the buildings were in bad repair, firewood had become scarce, but, above all, there were no longer enough orphans to warrant keeping it open.[11] Nome civil defense authorities, fearing that fresh vegetables might be in short supply in that area because of the war and uncertain ship movements, had urged Cunningham to put in the garden. While at the Springs, he also salvaged lumber for the church he planned to build at Marys Igloo that same summer.[12]

In late October, Cunningham and the men of Diomede, in their skin-boats, traveled from Nome to Wales for the crossing to their island home. The men had spent five months in Nome selling their ivory artifacts

Mission buildings at Pilgrim Hot Springs in 1972. *(National Park Service)*

and longshoring. At Wales a ship of the Alaska Steamship Company lay offshore waiting for a break in the weather to unload. Its captain was willing to take on board the Diomeders and Cunningham to transport them to the island for the winter. (Commercial ships, Coast Guard cutters, and Bureau of Indian Affairs ships, such as the *North Star*, frequently took the islanders, along with their boats and supplies, to the island.) No break in the weather came; instead, ice floes began to rock down from the Chukchi Sea. The captain, anxious for his ship, weighed anchor and steamed off for Seattle, leaving the Diomeders and their pastor stranded at Wales.

Cunningham had had a hard seven months in Nome and north of Nome. A touch of pneumonia had laid him low while he was at Marys Igloo. When he joined his flock at Wales for the trip to Diomede, he was still run-down. In spite of sleet and driving snow, he was determined to make the crossing to the island in one of the skinboats.

However, as the skinboat flotilla was about to set out for the island, he felt a chill; and, despite the cold, his temples were burning. A nurse, who happened to be at Wales at the time, took his temperature. It was 103°F. She absolutely forbade him to step into the boat, and ordered him to bed at once. His temperature continued to hover around 103, and he soon became delirious. A severe case of pneumonia was diagnosed. News of his sickness got around fast. In Fairbanks several U.S. Army bomber pilots requisitioned a Flying Fortress in hopes of being able to bring him to the Fairbanks hospital. But the weather was so unflyable that all government planes remained grounded.

William Munz, a skilled commercial pilot and owner of Munz Airline in Nome, set out to attempt a rescue, but a cloud ceiling of less than 200 feet and snow-laden headwinds turned him back. Up in Kotzebue Sig Wien heard the news. Immediately he dropped off his two charter passengers and headed toward Wales. He made it only as far as Shishmaref, where poor flying conditions forced him to spend the night. The next day, in spite of still very marginal weather, he was able to land at Wales. Cunningham was bundled into a sleeping bag and loaded on the plane. He hardly knew what was going on, but managed to murmur, "I knew you would come, Sig." Several hours later he was in the Nome hospital. When he felt better, he wanted to pay Wien for the mercy flight. Wien simply shrugged his shoulders. He and Cunningham had by then become close friends.[13]

Cunningham never did get to Diomede for the winter of 1942-43;

The *Crown City* stuck in the ice near Sledge Island. (Archives, University of Alaska-Fairbanks. Tom Christiansen collection)

instead, he spent it as pastor of Nome and the mission stations north of Nome. McHugh left Alaska in early December.[14]

In the late fall of 1942, the motor ship *Crown City*, with military cargo on board, was lying at anchor in the Nome roadstead, preparing to unload, when a violent storm blew up and made it necessary for her to seek shelter in the lee of Sledge Island, 25 miles west of Nome and five miles off the coast of Seward Peninsula. As she neared the island, she was impaled on an uncharted crag, and despite her military cargo Army officials wrote her off as lost after the Lomen Company, a Nome-based lightering company, assured them that both ship and cargo were beyond salvage.

That winter, as Cunningham was returning to Nome from Teller with his dog team, he swung out over the sea ice and boarded the *Crown City* to size up the situation. Upon his arrival in Nome, he went immediately to the Army base to assure Brigadier General Edwin W. Jones, commanding officer, that he would see to it that the cargo of the *Crown City* would be brought ashore if Jones would furnish the manpower. Jones and Cunningham flew out to the scene of the wreck in a small chartered plane. After looking things over for himself, and listening again to Cunningham's reasoning, Jones saw the feasibility of a salvage operation and supplied the necessary manpower.

Crews of soldiers and Eskimos, led by Cunningham, set to work. He himself ran the winch on the ship, hoisting cargo out of the hold and lowering it to the Eskimos down on the ice. With their dogsleds they hauled it to Army men waiting on the shore with tractors and sledges. After a few weeks of feverish activity, under truly adverse conditions, most of the military supplies were safely at the base.

One morning Cunningham called an abrupt halt to the whole operation and ordered all ashore at once, although a fair amount of desirable materiel still remained on board. The officer in charge of the Army detail protested, but Cunningham insisted, and all went ashore. Several hours later the ice around the ship began to break up.[15] Fortunately for all, Cunningham knew Bering Sea ice conditions by this time: how to listen to ice, and how to feel its movements, which he could do very well in the steel hull of the ship. He also seemed to have a sixth sense for ice behavior.

The military offered to pay Cunningham for his services, but he refused any financial reward — much as he could have used funds for his various missions. He saw the salvage operation as his patriotic duty.

One suspects, moreover, that he found it a great adventure and delighted in it. But he was generously thanked by the U.S. Army. On 29 May 1943, U.S. Army Brigadier General Frank L. Whittaker, Deputy Commander of the Alaska Defense Command, wrote him, "I am in receipt of a letter from the Commanding General in Nome, in which he mentions your invaluable services to his command in connection with the salvage operations on the Motor Ship *Crown City*. I wish to take this opportunity to express appreciation for this fine display of loyalty, courage, and helpfulness on your part. It is gratifying to find a person such as yourself who renders assistance where needed without prospect of material reward."

A week later Cunningham received a Citation of Commendation from Jones. The citation, dated 5 June 1943, praises Cunningham for having placed "his time and expert knowledge of the Seward Peninsula at the disposal of this command. On numerous occasions his help and advice have safeguarded the lives of troops and equipment and saved government funds...His close personal contact with the troops has had a beneficial influence upon their morale and his high standing in all the communities which he serves makes him the guiding spirit of those of all faiths. In true Christian spirit he has never accepted material compensation for his efforts beyond an occasional meal and night's lodging."[16]

Because of World War II, the Bureau of Indian Affairs was unable to find a teacher for Diomede for the 1943-44 school year. J. Sidney Rood, the Bureau's Nome representative, recommended to General Superintendent Claude M. Hirst in Juneau that Cunningham be appointed part-time teacher and supervisor of the cooperative store on the island. Rood suggested that Cunningham live in the school quarters for convenience's sake. For his services he was to be paid $105.90 per month.[17]

Hirst, in a letter dated 16 August 1943, asked Crimont whether such an arrangement would be agreeable to him. It was "perfectly agreeable" to Crimont, and Cunningham, too, was "perfectly willing" to cooperate with the Bureau, but he was reluctant to be fingerprinted as a condition for receiving a full civil service rating and a regular salary. "To be perfectly frank," he wrote Crimont on 16 October, "I prefer not to have the civil service rating nor the salary...I never did nor ever will expect any pay...I prefer to donate my services." Cunningham did, however, receive pay for his teaching. To Fitzgerald he wrote on 8 May 1944, "Enclosed please find your cut in the Diomede school wages."

In September Cunningham returned to Diomede on the *Waipio*, a commercial freighter which replaced the *North Star* that year. "The setup here," he wrote Crimont on 16 October, "suits me very well. I live in the school building. I turned one of the large rooms into a chapel for weekdays, and use the church only on Saturday night and Sunday. The school building has central heating and electric lights and is very handy. I teach from 9 a.m. to 12, 1 p.m. to 3 p.m., and from 6:30 to 9 (adults) in the evening. At least one hour of each period is given to catechism. The visiting and care of the sick means no added work as I used to do it anyhow. There are 36 children in the school of whom 34 are Catholic. The work concerning the co-op store is practically nil...The spirit of the island is good. Everyone seems to approve highly of the present arrangement."

Cunningham's last full winter on Little Diomede came to an end in early February 1944, when he flew to the mainland to make his annual eight-day retreat in Fairbanks. Bishop Fitzgerald, who was in residence there at the time, wrote on 28 February to the new Oregon Province Provincial, Leopold J. Robinson, S.J., concerning Cunningham. "I do not think it a violation of any confidence to state that his trip [to Fairbanks] was a life-saver in more ways than one. He had become 'fed up' on the Eskimos and just had to get away for a break...When Father Cunningham arrived here, he was in a state of nerves. He is in fine spirits again."

Apparently Cunningham gave satisfaction as a teacher on Diomede, for no sooner had he finished rendering the Bureau of Indian Affairs that service, than its Nome representative Rood wrote to Hirst requesting the latter's permission to hire Cunningham to operate the Bureau's supply boat during the summer of 1944. Cunningham did not, at first, seem to be in favor of operating the boat, which was to distribute essential supplies to the various Bureau schools located from Bering Strait to Nelson Island, but said he would do so if that were Bishop Crimont's wish. "Father Cunningham," wrote Fitzgerald to McElmeel, "wishes to make it plain that he wants only to do what Superiors decide, and does not want to carve out his own course of action. He is indifferent to what work he does."

Crimont, evidently swayed by the desire to help the government at a time when he thought no competent man could be found to operate the Bureau's boat, expressed his wish that Cunningham run it. Though "not at all enthusiastic about the job," according to Fitzgerald, who discussed it with him, Cunningham accepted.[18]

Despite his seeming reluctance, Cunningham appeared to be "quite happy to take on the work of managing the Indian Bureau boat," according to Fitzgerald, and from what we know about Cunningham and his experience with boats, it is likely that he looked forward to skippering the Bureau's boat, for he wrote enthusiastically that it was "perfectly safe, only three years old and has a splendid engine and suit of sails. It is a boat that could be sailed around the world without any danger... This summer will be the first time I ever travel in comfort."[19]

But Cunningham's newest adventure was not to be. For reasons unknown, Cunningham never did operate the Bureau's supply boat.[20] Instead, he was kept busy in Nome and outlying villages in a hectic spring and summer. In April he went by dog team to mission stations from Teller in the west to White Mountain in the east, with Marys Igloo, Pilgrim Springs, and Solomon in between. As in the previous two years he again helped the Army with its garden at Pilgrim Springs, and in August he worked on his new church at Marys Igloo.[21]

8 / U.S. Army Chaplain: 1945-1946

As early as 1941, Cunningham had hopes of becoming a military chaplain, as he mentioned in a letter to William G. Elliott in January 1942: "I was invited last year to be a military chaplain, but informed the major that everything would have to be taken up with Superiors. If ever you need any, I am ready," and later, justifying his request, "I just sort of figured it was the patriotic thing to do."[1]

Through Fitzgerald Cunningham asked Crimont for permission to enter the chaplain corps in 1943. Crimont responded that as much as he would like to grant the favor, he felt that it would not be proper to withdraw Cunningham from his work among the Eskimos.[2] Despite this negative answer, Cunningham, during his 1944 retreat, focused specially on whether or not he should continue to pursue a military chaplaincy. Convinced that he should, he discussed the matter with Fitzgerald, who then, upon Cunningham's request, wrote to Crimont, on 11 February, informing him that Cunningham had become "convinced that it was his duty to enter the armed forces as a chaplain." Fitzgerald relayed Cunningham's reasons for seeking a chaplaincy as follows: "1. It seems to him that the need of chaplains is greater now than the need of his remaining as missionary for the Eskimos. He does not want to give up permanently the work for which with so much labor and sacrifice he has prepared himself. The need of chaplains is only for a couple of years, and hence it is only a temporary employment. 2. He will return to the work for the Eskimos of the North just as soon as the war is over. 3. He feels that it is his duty to acquaint Your Excellency with his conviction that he would be able to do much good for the soldiers. He modestly asserts that from his past contact with the men at Nome, he is able to be of much spiritual help to them. He thinks that the missionary work could await his return. 4. He states that he is entirely resigned to God's will that is made known to him by the decision of Superiors. But he feels that he should make known again at the time of his retreat his dispositions of soul in regard to this matter."

Nine days later, on 20 February, Crimont replied that the Cunningham chaplaincy question would have to be settled "first and primarily" by Oregon Province Provincial Robinson. Should he grant Cunningham's request, he, Crimont, would do the same, but very reluctantly. Crimont feared that, if abandoned for a few years, the Seward Peninsula Catholic Eskimos would go over to the Lutherans. "Father Cunningham," wrote Crimont, "has proved by his contact with the soldiers in Nome and the results thereof that he can be a very efficient and influential Army chaplain. There is no denying it. But, an additional chaplain can be furnished from the U.S., whereas a missionary for the Eskimos to replace Father Cunningham cannot be furnished from any place in the world."[3]

Shortly thereafter Crimont again wrote to Fitzgerald, "All is now settled about [Cunningham's] desire to be an Army chaplain. I consider the case closed."[4] And on 28 February, Fitzgerald wrote to Robinson, "Father Tom has withdrawn his application."

On 27 April Cunningham wrote to Fitzgerald, who had told him two months previously to "forget the military chaplain business," that he would like "you and all Superiors to understand that any efforts on the part of the military to have me in the Army have neither my sympathy nor support. I know your mind in the matter and long ago made up my mind accordingly. I ignore, and intend to ignore, my own personal leanings in the matter."

One would think — in light of the correspondence just cited — that the "military chaplain business" was settled, once and for all, but Cunningham could not ignore his personal leanings all that easily, nor could he ignore the pressure from the military, toward which he was very favorably disposed. And, when he really wanted something, he proved himself a man at once resolute and resourceful. Besides, he had his sympathetic supporters, not only in the military, but among his fellow Jesuits.

A highly hopeful Cunningham wrote to Crimont on 29 August 1944: "You have gotten letters of this trend already from me, but this time it looks like something that will satisfy both of us. Yes, it's about being an Army chaplain." It is easy to imagine Crimont's reaction to that opener.

But what Cunningham proposed was a plan whereby he could become a chaplain and still continue his missionary work: to be chaplain to a local Search and Rescue Squadron.

By mid-1944 the Lend-Lease Act passed by Congress on 11 March 1941 was making itself powerfully felt in Nome. In accordance with the Act, planes by the thousands were being ferried to Russia via Nome. Given the volume of air traffic and the extraordinary, challenging flying conditions in that part of the world owing to unstable, adverse weather patterns and inhospitable terrain, military authorities deemed it advisable to organize a Search and Rescue Squadron consisting of as many local people as possible. This squadron was made to order for Cunningham. "This is country and ice that I know," he wrote Crimont, "and they want me as chaplain." To make Crimont more receptive to his proposal, he added, "Quite possibly some of my Eskimo parishioners will be in it. I have thought the matter over, prayed considerably about it, consulted with Fr. Lafortune and the conclusion seems to be that I join."

Knowing well Crimont's basic objection to his becoming a chaplain, Cunningham took great care in building his case. He went on to assure Crimont that he would be based in Nome — with his work confined exclusively to his own territory — and that he would always be free during the winter months to spend time with his Eskimo congregations. "Being an Army chaplain will help rather than hinder the work with the Natives. The Natives will not suffer by it, and they will be proud of their pastor." Then he continued to load the balance in his favor: "It will do me much good personally, because I feel, after prayer on the matter, that it's work I can do well, that will not interfere too much with what I am doing now, and that my knowledge of local conditions, climate, ice movements, etc. will be of great value in saving numbers of lives. Most important of all, these lads need a priest."

After asking Crimont to give his request "careful consideration" and to wire him his "yes" or "no," Cunningham concluded his letter, "Be assured, however, Bishop Crimont, that in this matter, as in all matters connected with our mission, I am always ready to abide by any decision you might make." At the foot of this letter, Lafortune wrote, and signed, "I endorse all what is written in the above." Cunningham was shrewd in communicating Lafortune's endorsement in this way to Crimont, for he knew that Crimont considered Lafortune a premier missionary endowed with sound judgment. Bernard R. Hubbard, S.J., the famed "Glacier Priest" and Crimont's esteemed friend, also wrote at this time and in the same vein on Cunningham's behalf.[5]

Cunningham had little doubt that this was his last opportunity to obtain permission from Superiors to apply for a chaplaincy. He was aware that Fitzgerald, who earlier favored his getting a chaplaincy, was by now adamantly opposed to the idea, because he had come to consider Cunningham "a rather restless sort of character," and feared that his "drinking" would be his "entire ruination" in the military.[6] Crimont was now in his 87th year. Cunningham knew that the end could not be far off, and that Fitzgerald would then succeed Crimont as bishop in charge. He knew, too, that Provincial Robinson was against his entering the service.

Given this state of affairs, Cunningham saw clearly that Crimont was his one and only hope, so, in his plan as outlined in his 29 August letter, he added two pages of postscript, repeating the same arguments in favor of his obtaining a chaplaincy, and urging Crimont, "If you agree to this Army proposal, and I sincerely hope you do, please wire me."

Cunningham, who had made it plain six months earlier that he did not want to "carve out his own course of action," was now pretty well doing just that. He could be persuasive. By early September, he had his answer from Crimont. "Many thanks," he wrote Crimont on the 12th, "for your kind letter of Sept. 5th and your approval of the Army chaplaincy, in the *limited* [emphasis added] capacity."[7]

Why did Crimont give his approval in spite of the fact that the Oregon Province Provincial and his own coadjutor bishop strongly opposed the Army chaplaincy for Cunningham? Was the mind of the venerable old bishop failing? It is well known that he was fully alert to the end of his life. Was he "taken in" by Cunningham? He was too astute a man for that. And how did he get around his own position that "the question of U.S. Army chaplaincy has to be settled first and primarily by Father Provincial"?

Even if Cunningham's arguments and the Lafortune and Hubbard endorsements weighed with Crimont, they were not the determining factors. One consideration, one word alone, "limited," tipped the balance in Cunningham's favor. Once Crimont was convinced that his military activity would be limited to the Seward Peninsula area only, and limited in such a way that he would have some months free each year to devote to the Eskimos under his care, he saw his way clear to approval. He believed that, given these circumstances — under which Cunningham would not be removed from missionary work in Alaska — he would be in compliance with the policy agreed upon by him and Oregon Province

Provincials, namely, that the bishop had something to say as to where and how Jesuits served within Alaska, but only the provincial could assign a man to, or withdraw him from, Alaska.

Cunningham received his commission in the U.S. Army on 11 January 1945, and was ordered to active duty and authorized to wear the Army uniform on the 22nd. "I can well remember the evening," wrote Anable, pastor of Nome at the time, "when he first donned the uniform of an officer of the U.S. [Army] Air Force to go out to the military base and be sworn in. At that time he stated, 'I have never wanted anything so much as I want this.'" According to Anable, "Father Tom literally became enamored with the military. Nome had both an Air Force base and an Army base; and those, along with the military hospital, were his favorite places."[8]

First Lieutenant Cunningham left Nome on 24 January for Fort Devens, Massachusetts, where he arrived on 9 February to attend Chaplain School. On 28 February he was honorably discharged from the Alaska Territorial Guard, in which he had served since 15 September 1942. The discharge document described his character as "excellent" and his service as "a definite and praiseworthy contribution to the defense of the territory."

At Fort Devens Cunningham successfully completed courses in infiltration, map and aerial photo reading, and marksmanship, as well as in military chaplaincy. As a rifleman he attained the ranking of "expert." After graduation from Chaplain School on the feast of St. Patrick, 17 March, he was assigned as chaplain to the 1469th Army Air Forces Base Unit, Air Transport Command, Nome.

Back in Nome after the war, he told Anable a Fort Devens incident that almost cost him his military career. One day two chaplains were telling "dirty stories," and, as on previous similar occasions, Cunningham voiced his disapproval of their conduct. When, after fair warning, they refused to change the subject, he cracked their heads together, giving them both mild concussions. Word of this reached the commandant of Chaplain School. Cunningham was spared a court-martial only by the intervention of Archbishop Richard J. Cushing of Boston.[9] Once again Cunningham proved to be a man of direct, decisive action.

Cunningham, though himself rough-hewn and worldly-wise, had a low tolerance for obscenity and profanity. Anable recalled how Cunningham discouraged profane, unbecoming language among the Nome soldiers, officers not excepted. He would fine them on the spot if he heard them swearing, and the severity of the fine was determined by the severity of the language abuse. Toward the end of his assignment in Nome, he put on a banquet — "unlike anything Nome had ever seen" — to which he invited all the culprits. He paid the whole bill with the money generated by the fines.[10] Sometime later a certain colonel said to him, "Ah, yes! You're the priest who taught me to quit swearing."[11] The men did not seem to take it amiss that Cunningham censured them for unbecoming language.

As a chaplain he received a salary of $202 per month. Of this, he sent Bishop Fitzgerald as close to $150 as he was able, but sometimes he sent the whole of his salary ("enclosed is my entire salary for July, including raise"). He also tried to give small donations to Anable in Nome.[12] No matter what his own needs might be, or what the source of his income was, Cunningham and money never did get along well together. Before it had a chance to get warm in his pocket, it was gone.

From 16 to 28 September 1945 he was at Mather Field, California, awaiting an assignment in the Pacific Division, and on the 29th, he arrived at Hickam Field, Hawaii, where on 12 November he was promoted to the rank of captain. He had requested an assignment somewhere in the Pacific Theater, hoping to visit New Zealand and his aging parents, whom he had not seen since 1924. He had almost gone to teach in Australia in 1930, and had discussed the possibility of going home with Fitzgerald in 1944, since his father was quite old, "over 86 years," but at that time it was not yet the practice for Jesuits in Alaska to make trips "outside" because of old age, sickness, or death in the family.[13]

Therefore, Cunningham's next assignment, in mid-November, must have caused his heart to leap for joy, because he was told to report to Tontouta Air Base on New Caledonia, a scant thousand miles from his family.

When he arrived on New Caledonia, he was granted a seven-day temporary duty leave and was authorized, on 19 November 1945, to make an immediate round trip — priority air travel — to Auckland, New Zealand. From there he traveled on his own to Mosgiel to visit his parents, two of his brothers, and nieces and nephews, and then went on to Gore to spend some time with his brother John and family.

While in Gore, Cunningham was interviewed by the local newspaper, a lengthy article about him and his work in Alaska appearing in the 30 November issue. After commenting on the Eskimo population of Little Diomede, he said that "the white population is strong and undivided in religion, nationality, and politics — it consists of myself." On 13

December 1945, the newspaper *Zealandia* also carried an article about him and his missionary work, along with a striking photo of him in uniform posing with Bishop James M. Liston, his former seminary rector.

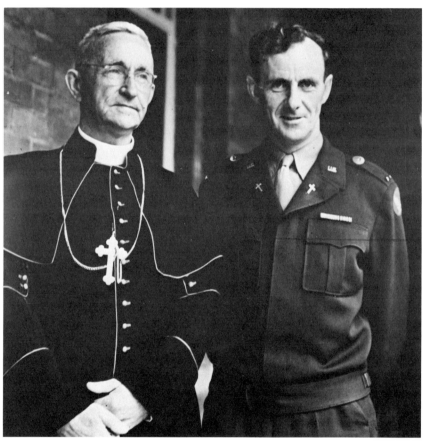

This photo of Father Tom with his former seminary Rector, Bishop James M. Liston, who later became archbishop of the Auckland diocese, appeared in the 13 December 1945 issue of the newspaper *Zealandia*. *(Oregon Province Archives)*

On 19 December, Cunningham's odyssey "down under" took him on a side trip to Brisbane, Australia, "for the purpose of coordinating chaplain activities." For the Christmas season he was back at the Tontouta Air Base. "It is dreadfully hot here," he wrote Fitzgerald on 3 January 1946, "and it's considerable of a job to keep 500 home-hungry soldiers reasonably satisfied. In fact, it cannot be done. Christmas was quiet and rather unusual under a tropical sun."

Early in January, Cunningham was granted a ten-day emergency leave of absence to be at the bedside of his "dying" father. (Mr. Cunningham died two years later, in April 1948.[14]) As a show of sympathy for him on this "sad" occasion, and as a memento of his visit to his home town, the people of the Mosgiel parish had a formal card printed and addressed to him: "Rev. and Dear Father, It is with great pleasure, and with gratitude to God, that we welcome you. The parishioners look on you as one of God's Heroes and feel very proud of you and the Missionary work you are doing in His Vineyard. We pray that God will grant you health and strength to work for many more years amongst your beloved people — the Eskimos. Our prayers will always be with you, and the memory of your visit here, which we are celebrating tonight, will be a treasured one throughout our lives. We extend to you all good wishes, and beg to remain your sincere friends."

After not seeing his family for over two decades, Cunningham saw them twice in less than two months. Later, when he was back in Nome, his friends accused him — good-naturedly, to be sure — of having joined the Army just to get a trip home at taxpayers' expense.[15]

In late February, Cunningham was transferred from New Caledonia to Manila. On the 26th he wrote Fitzgerald that "all ATC [Air Transport Command] chaplains [were declared] surplus last month and they sent them all back to the U.S. except Fr. Biasoli and myself, the reason given being that we were not yet eligible for discharge, and, furthermore, they keep overseas those with the highest efficiency rating — which is very flattering but still annoying."

Cunningham's Manila tour of duty, which lasted only about three weeks, included side trips to Honolulu, Saipan, and Guam. Then came a ten-day stay in Japan, and a four-months tour, from 29 March to 20 July, in Korea. On 11 June, he wrote to Fitzgerald, "Life here is very busy and conditions rugged, what with bad weather, unfriendly Koreans, dissatisfied soldiers, etc. But from the point of view of the Church, the results are really worthwhile." After Korea he returned to the Atsugi Army Air Base in Japan for five weeks, at which time he made a ten-day retreat with the Jesuits in Tokyo.[16]

So much for Cunningham's assurances to Crimont that, if he became a military chaplain, he would be based in Nome, working exclusively in his own mission territory, free to spend an occasional month visiting his Native congregations who would be proud of their chaplain pastor. So much, too, for the valuable assistance he would render the Nome-based Search and Rescue Squadron because of his expertise in that area's weather and ice conditions. But, Crimont never knew about Chaplain Cunningham's extra-Alaskan, Pacific Theater peregrinations, for he died on 20 May 1945.

However, Bishop Fitzgerald had kept up an unrelenting letterwriting campaign throughout the spring and summer of 1946 to get Cunningham, whose absence he considered "a grievous loss to the missions," out of the service and back to his work among the Eskimos. Fitzgerald built his case primarily on two premises: that Cunningham had unique qualifications as a missionary in Alaska because of his thorough knowledge of the Eskimo language, and that he had been promised (so Fitzgerald mistakenly thought) to be stationed in the Nome area. Great was Fitzgerald's surprise when he learned from the Military Ordinariate in Washington that there was "no documentary evidence in the file of Father Cunningham to the effect that he was to serve only in Alaska," and that "Father Cunningham was sent to the Pacific only because of his personal request for such an assignment."[17]

Even after Fitzgerald learned that the Military Ordinariate and the Office of Chief of Chaplains had acted in good faith all along, he continued to plead for Cunningham's early release from the service. Military Vicar Francis Cardinal Spellman, and the Military Ordinariate, and Chief of Chaplains Major General Luther Miller immediately set the wheels in motion for an early release. To Fitzgerald, Miller wrote, on 16 June, "I can well appreciate the value that you place in Chaplain Cunningham and want you to know that his services to the military chaplaincy have been splendid. We will be sorry to lose him."

Cunningham cooperated fully with his bishop and military authorities in expediting his early separation. To Fitzgerald he wrote from Korea on 11 June, "I hope sincerely you have gotten a favorable reply from the War Department, as I am as anxious to be back in Alaska as I hope you are to have me there."

Cunningham returned stateside, to Fort Lewis, Washington, in early September, 1946. On the 9th, after receiving his appointment in the Army Officers' Reserve Corps, he was released from active duty to take accumulated leave,[18] and was officially separated from active service as of 11 October with a "superior" rating, making him one of the very few retiring officers to receive a rating above "excellent."[19]

9 / Nome: 1946-1947
King Island: 1947-1950

Cunningham returned to Alaska in the latter part of September, 1946, and went immediately to Little Diomede, where he "found little change," according to the island diary. However, he was back in Nome by early October to assume charge of the Nome parish and all of Seward Peninsula during the temporary absence of Anable.

He was busier than usual during his first week in Nome, with two deaths, one funeral, two marriages, and one baptism. He had not forgotten the Eskimo language, for he wrote Fitzgerald that he "preached in Eskimo at one of the Masses and managed OK. Had begun to learn Korean, but desisted when I noticed I was mixing it up with Eskimo."

He also wrote that he needed some money: "If you have any of the money I sent you, I would appreciate about $400. It will take about that much to get through the winter as it's kind of starting from scratch, and there is repair work to be done. If you cannot send $400, I can get by with less."[1]

It was a more or less typical Cunningham procedure to hand over to Superiors any large sum of money that he received; then, later on when he needed money, to ask them to return some of it, to "nibble at it," as he put it.[2] First, he would ask for a specific amount, then quickly modify his request by saying if that amount, or even less, were not available, he would still be able to manage somehow. Knowing Cunningham's own generosity and easily-satisfied nature, Superiors granted his requests for money whenever possible.

During the winter of 1946-47, Cunningham tended his Eskimo flock in and out of Nome. He spent a fair amount of time at Marys Igloo and Teller. In early February, he returned to Diomede, where he imme-

Aerial view of King Island. The village of Ukivok hangs center front near the water. (Louis L. Renner, S.J., collection)

diately set up a regular Mass and catechism schedule. Both adults and children attended faithfully. Of the almost one hundred people on the island, all but nine were Catholic by this time.

March brought with it favorable weather, good hunting — and a great day for "all the igloos of Little Diomede Island," St. Patrick's Day. No saint's feast day was so much celebrated on Diomede as that of St. Patrick, in whose honor Father Thomas Patrick Cunningham had composed a hymn in Eskimo, which the Diomeders sang with gusto and a "brogue all their own."[3]

In June, Cunningham took advantage of the beautiful weather to paint the inside of the church, the floor, and the benches. He ordered enough green asphalt shingles to cover the roof and enough brick-finish tarpaper to cover the outside of the church. "That should make the building good for another 20 years," he wrote in the Diomede diary, and indeed it did, for the church was not replaced with a new one until 1978.

Cunningham left Diomede in late June for Teller, where he planned to spend the summer. Later that month, Lafortune arrived in Nome from King Island. He was no longer the rugged little giant that he had been for over four decades in Alaska. Though he had not been sick during his last winter on King Island, he had lost much of his strength. It is thought that he had had a stroke. Around mid-July, Lafortune, while saying Mass, collapsed at the altar of St. Joseph's Church in Nome. Anable was in Fairbanks at the time, so Cunningham came from Teller to administer the last rites to him and take him to the Nome hospital. In late July, he and Anable took Lafortune to Fairbanks, and Cunningham then returned to Nome to serve as temporary pastor. At this time, Alaska Mission Superior Paul C. Deschout, S.J., was making his visitation of Nome, and one of his official acts was to assign Cunningham to King Island.[4]

King Island, some 90 miles northwest of Nome and 35 miles off the coast of the Seward Peninsula, resembles Little Diomede in many respects. Two and a half miles long, a mile and a half wide, with an elevation of 1196 feet, it is a bit bigger than Diomede, though not as high. Its longer axis is oriented east and west, and sheer cliffs ring the island except for slight embayments in the southern and northwestern shorelines where the slopes are somewhat less steep. The island has no beaches, and granite boulders rounded off by wave action provide only three boat landing places.

The village, abandoned since 1966, was built on the south side of the

Ukivok village on King Island, 1937. When Father Tom first went to King Island in 1947, he lived in the house Father Bernard Hubbard had built for himself ten years earlier — the one to the left of the white house in front of the church. After the Hubbard party left Kind Island in 1938, Father Lafortune moved into the Hubbard house and used his own former house — the one next to the Hubbard House — as a weekday chapel. In the spring of 1948, Father Tom dismantled two of the Hubbard party houses and with the salvaged lumber built living quarters for himself on the left end of the chapel. (Photo by Bernard R. Hubbard, S.J. Courtesy of Archives University of Santa Clara)

island on a rock slide 200 feet wide, with a pitch of about 40 degrees to the sea, making the King Islanders true cliff-dwellers.[5] About fifty yards east of the village a small, precipitous stream drains most of the upland plateau through a gully. This stream provided water for the village during the summer and fall; snow was melted during the rest of the year.

A quarter of a mile east of the village, there is a large double-chambered cave. This natural, year-round deepfreeze, in which surplus meat from successful hunts could be preserved against lean days sure to come, always tipped the balance in favor of the people's staying on the island, whenever the question of abandoning it was raised. Meat in the cave was a matter of life and death in the days when a few walrus or seals in storage made the difference between eating or starving. By the middle of the present century, however, modern methods of distributing and preserving non-Native foods had stripped the cave of much of its former importance.

King Island was officially "discovered" by Captain James Cook of the English Royal Navy in 1778, who named it after his executive officer, Lieutenant James King. Its Eskimo inhabitants, however, called it and their village on it, *ugiuvuk* (Ukivok on present-day maps), meaning "big winter" or "winter's home." This name reflects the traditional yearly cycle of the King Islanders, who spent the winters in isolation on their tiny granite isle and the summers traveling and trading along the mainland coasts. Like the Little Diomeders, the King Islanders were called *imaangmiut*, "the people of the open water," by the mainland Eskimos.

Most white people who have visited King Island have described it in the austerest of terms: "a high, rocky mass, with steep cliffs on all sides...a most inhospitable place, in calm weather usually swathed in mist, in clear weather windy...a melancholy rock...a more forsaken, wildly-desolate, oppressingly-isolated isle, wrapped in cold deathliness, cannot be imagined...the loneliest spot in the world, the paradise of the birds and the storms." But the King Islanders, to whom it was home for countless generations, saw it as a true paradise also for man. Almost everything needed to sustain a comfortable way of life was provided by the island and the sea around it. The upland plateau and cliffs provided a variety of edible plants and countless birds and their eggs. The surrounding waters abounded in fish, crabs, shrimp, seals, walrus, and polar bears.

The first entry in Cunningham's hand in the King Island diary, dated 14

October 1947, reads, "The *Bozo* came today with 17 longshoremen and Fr. T. Cunningham, who replaces Fr. Lafortune." Lafortune was the first to master the language of the King Islanders and convert them all to Catholicism in the early part of the century during their summers in Nome; and it was he who built the church on their island, in 1929; and it was he who introduced Cunningham to the Seward Peninsula area Eskimo apostolate in 1935.

Lafortune died on 22 October 1947, news of which reached Cunningham via radio, and the following day he wrote in the diary, "He was one giant of a man, exemplary Jesuit and good friend." And the friendship was mutual. In the course of the eleven years during which the two worked together, Lafortune, who set very high standards for missionaries and missionary work among the Eskimos, had come to know and appreciate Cunningham's sterling qualities as a priest and missionary. This appreciation meant more to Cunningham than that of anyone else, and more than outweighed all negative criticism of him and his work, no matter from what quarter it came.

Cunningham's services on Diomede had been so satisfactory to the Bureau of Indian Affairs that the Bureau, which had built a school on King Island in 1929, the same year that Lafortune built the church, recruited Cunningham as teacher for King Island, since they had been unable to fill the position. As on Diomede, he chose to live in the schoolhouse so as not to have to commute from the top of the village to the bottom several times a day. He found the schoolhouse "comfortable," and built an altar in the classroom for weekday Masses. "Daily Mass attendance excellent," he recorded in the diary. Church-State relationships on King Island were harmonious and mutually satisfactory. He had 62 pupils from a population of 198.[6]

In addition to teaching school, Cunningham continued Lafortune's long-established tradition of regular and systematic catechizing, of visiting the sick, and of sharing in village life, but unlike Lafortune, he also joined the men in hunting. "On Wednesday and Saturday," he wrote, "I hunt in the afternoons, as I need to eat too. All hunting is done on moving ice, and it is sometimes dangerous and always cold and miserable."[7]

He really did not have to hunt. The King Islanders faithfully provided Lafortune with all the meat he needed (he gave them "white man grub" in return), and they would surely have done the same for Cunningham, for, indeed, he recorded from time to time in the diary that he was given meat.

Cunningham hunted not so much because he needed meat — which, of course, he did — but because he needed to hunt. He was a hunter at heart, and according to the King Islanders, a good one. Aloysius Pikonganna, master ivory carver and expert hunter himself, said of Cunningham, "He's tough man, that one! He go hunt on ice, just like us. All alone. He come back [with] something everytime. Ahhhh! Father Tom!"[8]

It did not take Cunningham long to discover that the King Island variant of Inupiaq Eskimo was different enough from that spoken on Diomede "to make conversation difficult at times," and he once remarked that "the language here differs enough from the Diomede one to just about make a new dialect...If I use Diomede words or expressions, I am corrected with tact and firmness."[9]

During his first years on Diomede, Cunningham had faithfully devoted many hours to the study of the language, which, he once wrote, "is very difficult to learn without any dictionary, grammar or literature of any kind." He had to translate into Eskimo the prayers, hymns, catechism, Sunday gospels, and the commentaries on these. While learning the language and making these translations, he prepared a rudimentary grammar and a dictionary, which, after two years, was "about 1000 pages," and, after three, he had a dictionary "completed, containing all the English words translatable into Eskimo. There are perhaps seven thousand of them."[10]

Frances A. Ross, an anthropologist, who saw his notebooks later at Barrow, wrote, "From the bookshelf above the wireless, he now removed two dusty, thick notebooks and handed them to me. As I turned the typewritten pages and glanced at the careful corrections, I could not repress a gasp. 'What's the matter?' he asked. 'Why, Father! I'm full of awe — this is most scholarly!' That he shrugged off, although confessing diffidently that 'it was fierce work at times.' One notebook contained his analysis of the Eskimo dialects of northwest Alaska. With a scholar's thorough care and detail he had developed a serious study of the difficult language, conjugating transitive and intransitive verbs, together with their positive and negative forms; declining nouns for common and irregular endings. The second notebook, arranged as a dictionary, listed hundreds of Eskimo words with their English meanings."[11]

Cunningham's linguistic legacy also includes a printed 108-page phrase book, which was produced for the use of Air Force personnel serving in the

Arctic. It was sponsored by the Alaskan Air Command, and bears the title *Phonetic Guide to the Eskimo Language.*[12] I asked Dr. Lawrence D. Kaplan, University of Alaska-Fairbanks Inupiaq specialist, to evaluate Cunningham's linguistic work, and after pointing out shortcomings in it, he concluded, "Cunningham's work, nevertheless, represents an important early contribution to the documentation of Seward Peninsula Inupiaq. Despite the shortcomings [that I have cited], the contribution of men such as Cunningham who broke ground early on in the recording of native languages deserves to be acknowledged."[13]

As his days on King Island stretched into weeks, and weeks into months, Cunningham faithfully recorded in the King Island diary information concerning weather, hunting, ice conditions; church, school, catechism attendance; the health of the people, births, baptisms, deaths. Almost every facet of King Island life sooner or later found its way into the diary. A selection of entries, arranged in chronological sequence, for the half year mid-October 1947 through mid-April 1948 weaves the following rich tapestry of life on King Island:

"October — Romeo committed suicide this morning. Shot himself...Baptized one baby...The men are getting a few seals every day...Rather heavy storm raging. Waves seem to be about 100 feet up on the rocks...John Kokuluk rather sick.

"November—Blessed one house!...All Masses well attended. The singing is very good...There were a lot of walrus sporting around the other day...Baptized baby of Alvana today...Hunting fair. Not much heavy ice as yet...One or two sick children...A few oogruks and seals taken...Freezing rain makes all the stairs dangerous.

"December — A snowslide on the creek today nearly ended the life of Xavier Siloak. He was down at sea level, when the snow slid down and took him over the rocks and into the water, but he kept his head and wormed his way up through the snow...Gave last sacraments to Kasignac...Weather has been terrible. North wind, below zero and mountains of snow...Aolaranna brought me a large chunk of walrus meat. The gift was most welcome...The wife of Ignatius Ailec died this morning...One polar bear was gotten today...Health of everyone remains good...There is a spirit of Christmas in the air...Christmas was splendid...Children very interested in crib...All the women had new parkas and the men dressed in their Sunday best. The collection at midnight was $82...The snow is mountainous...Very cold weather all week.

"January — The new year [1948] brought us the coldest day so far. 20° below and a gale of hurricane proportions. Consequently, the church was very cold, so cold, in fact, that the wine crystallized in the chalice, and the chalice and ciborium were almost too cold to touch. In spite of all this, the crowd were all there, and the day was pleasant enough...Beautiful calm day...Two oogruks were taken today...Health of everyone good...Hunting has been very good. Yesterday at least 20 seals and 3 oogruks were taken...Fishing through the ice also is good...Outside the church door there is at least 16 feet of snow...Temperature reached 20 above today...Temp. hit the low spot suddenly again. Drop of 38° in three hours...Terrific snowstorm all day...Daughter born this morning to Payenna and wife...There is a clear sweep of snow from the store down to the ice, covering houses and all...Wind at least 50 mph...The bell tower is completely under...Two baptisms today...Hunting poor, fishing fair.

"February — Two polar bears killed today...Mild weather all week...Ice terrible. South current very strong and pressure ridges are formed all along the shore...Move up this week to little chapel. It makes a nice home. It is easy to go down and teach in the school for a few hours every day...For the first time this season the church couldn't be used. There's a terrific north wind and the draft forces the smoke down, puts out the fire, and then the fire re-ignites with a mild explosion. The building is soon filled with gas. The same thing happened all day to a lesser extent in the house, but it was not unbearable. The temp. has been around − 20 all day and the wind over 70 mph...100% attendance at Mass this morning...Weather has been miserable all week. Hunting poor, health of everyone good...A plane came today and dropped some mail and a note saying I have to go to Nome as there is no priest there...Climbed up on the island today and notice it's impossible for a plane to land anywhere there. My only bet is to be out on smooth floating ice when the plane comes...Went out on the ice towards the west, and there are lots of landing places about a mile offshore...The people are not pleased with the idea of the priest leaving...They are praying for bad weather, or anything to put off the plane. One hundred percent turn out for both Masses and Benediction.

"March — We have been going out to smooth, moving ice all week, but no sign of plane. The weather has been perfect too...Hunting has been very poor this last week...A plane flew over and dropped mail. We were on a good spot on moving ice, but he made no attempt to land.

It seems the Nome situation is under control and I can remain here...Ilana ran his spear through the fleshy part of his left arm, but the wound is responding to treatment nicely...Anaruk had a narrow escape yesterday. The chunk of ice he was riding turned turtle. He lost his rifle, bag, and Aalic's kayak. The kayak was later recovered badly broken...For the first time since last October the shade temperature is above freezing...Thank God there has been very little sickness this year...St. Patrick's Day. Probably the stormiest day of the whole year. Temp. well below zero and north wind in gusts up to 75 mph as measured on windcharger...Pullach got the first white whale of the season today. Each family, including myself, has a good share of the meat and muktuk...Great excitement today. A plane came over and without any preliminary circling landed on smooth, slowly moving ice at the west side of the island...When they took off, their field was already beginning to break up...Holy Thursday. It's really too stormy to be hunting, and the men are spending a lot of time in the church. All last night and today the ice is roaring louder than usual. It resembles in sound a lot of freight cars moving slowly...Easter Sunday. The weather rejoiced with Our Lord's Resurrection. Church nicely decorated, singing excellent, people devout.

"April — Baby boy was born to Paul Nataanga and Aneana...The store is out of coffee, tea, lard; short on sugar and no baking powder or soda. Thank goodness I can get along very easily without any of the above items...Mayac and Kokuluk finished their boat and had it blessed today...Hunting nil, fishing fair...Snow is melting a little...Two men had a narrow squeak on the ice today. They went rather far out and the moving ice started to break up. After dark they lighted matches and we could see where they were. We helped out on shore with lantern, rifle shots and much shouting. It was 3 a.m. before they were really safe...Snow diminishing gradually."

There was great excitement on King Island on 20 April 1948, when a plane flew over and successfully dropped supplies and mail from about 2000 feet. Late April snows more than neutralized earlier melting. But the hunting was good. In one three-day period, over 30 oogruks were taken. The oogruk (more properly spelled "ugruk"), or bearded seal, was especially prized. It was by far the biggest of the seals hunted by the King Islanders, with males weighing up to 700 pounds. Its meat was not highly regarded as food for human beings, but its skin was considered the best for making the tough, waterproof soles of the Eskimo

Nome in 1948. St. Joseph's Church can be seen in front of the old Holy Cross Hospital, middle right. *(Photo by William A. Shepherd. Dorothy Jean Ray collection)*

boot, or mukluk, and for covering kayaks. Harpoon lines, and rope in general, were commonly made of ugruk rawhide.

Hunting during May and June yielded all the meat and skins needed, plus a fair crop of ivory for carving. The King Island men always ranked among the foremost ivory carvers in western Alaska, and spent much of their indoor time on the island carving artifacts. These found a ready market in Nome, especially among tourists.[14]

On 4 June Cunningham wrote in the diary, "I go out in one of the boats mainly because I don't like being the only man in the village," and the next day his first winter on King Island came to an end when he went to Wales with the King Islanders. Despite adverse ice conditions, three boatloads of men made the 55-mile crossing for supplies. Cunningham went along, hoping for an opportunity to get to Little Diomede, but with none presenting itself, he went to Teller where he had his own boat, which he then decided to use for the trip. But it was an arduous undertaking, and, because of the dense pack ice and a succession of storms, it took him from 20 June to 8 July to work his way from Teller to Diomede. He spent almost four weeks there before returning to Nome on 5 August. The next day he wrote to his former classmate and Oregon Province Provincial, Harold O. Small, S.J., that "everything is normal [on Diomede]. The Eskimos are kind of annoyed I cannot spend all the time there, but they understand."

Cunningham spent the next two and half months in Nome. This seems to have been a relatively easy, quiet period for him. With the King Islanders, he left Nome on a government ship for his second winter on King Island on 18 October. The crossing was a rough one; and, when they reached the island the next day, they had to land and unload everything on the north side. The people climbed over the top of the island to the village, and, when the seas calmed, freight and belongings were brought around to the village in skinboats.

The previous spring, Cunningham, with the help of some of the villagers, had dismantled two of the houses Hubbard and his crew had built for themselves when they spent the 1937-38 winter on the island. On 21 October, with the salvaged lumber, Cunningham and three of the men began to build an addition to the small weekday chapel to serve as his living quarters. Dried grass was used in the walls as insulation. For lighting he made one good windcharger out of three old ones.

"The New Year came and went with a minimum of noise and much happiness," wrote Cunningham in the diary on 5 January 1949. The following day, however, he began the diary entry, "Bad news today. Three of our young men floated away northward on the ice. They were seen to be in danger but could not be aided. They are Gregory Ayac, Raphael Pariena, and Lawrence Mazenna. The first two are unmarried, the latter has three children at Akulurak [St. Mary's Mission boarding school]. His wife died last year. The temp. is a little below zero. Fairly calm."

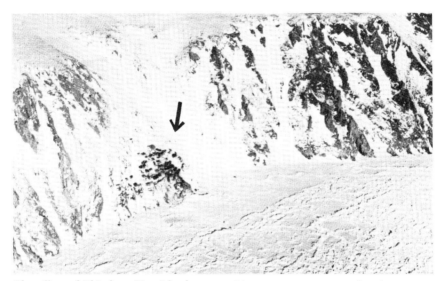

The village of Ukivok on King Island. *(Reprinted from ALASKA SPORTSMAN®, February 1969)*

On Friday morning, 7 January, Cunningham sent a wire on his recently acquired radio transmitter to the commanding officer of the Army in Nome requesting the military to help in locating the lost men and to drop food and sleeping bags to them.[15] The C.O. replied immediately that as soon as weather permitted men would take off to begin the search.

"Friday, Saturday and today have been terrible," wrote Cunningham on Sunday, 9 January. "The worst blizzard of the winter has been blowing, though the temp. is above zero. Visibility is nil. There is no word of the missing men from Wales, Teller or Diomede. Had they reached the mainland, we should have word by now. The Army regrets that they cannot do anything, as the weather is terrible in Nome too. . . The people here are losing hope for the lost men."

On Monday, the weather improved, and an Army plane took off to search. For the next four days, Army planes kept up the search without finding a trace of the three missing men. The search was called off on Friday the 14th, eight days after the three drifted away. Wires were sent to the Army units which had helped, thanking them for their part in the search. "Those outfits certainly did their best for us," wrote Cunningham in the diary.

Just when he and the King Islanders had given up all hope for the safety of the lost hunters, word came over the radio that fairly fresh tracks of three men had been seen on the mainland some distance southwest of Shishmaref. That was on Saturday, 22 January. On Wednesday, the 26th, a wire sent by James Brooks, the Weather Bureau observer at Wales, reached King Island. Brooks radioed the contents of a note that had been written with frostbitten hands by Gregory Ayac. One of the men was alive! After a harrowing experience of 14 days and 342 miles of treacherous ice, he had found refuge in a small shelter cabin on the mainland near Shishmaref, where he was rescued by Arnold Olanna, who, with characteristic Eskimo calm, asked him, "You King Island boy?" "Yes," answered Ayac.

The note was carried to Wales by Elliot Olanna, Arnold's brother. Addressed to Cunningham and Ayac's mother, the note described the ordeal:

"One man just found me yesterday at 12 p.m. at this Sinrazat shelter cabin after I had slept four days through. I stop there after I walk for three days out in the country. I got to land on 17th last week.

"When we first got away from island we were in good [shape] all of us. And next day comes it was snowing and damp and that day and then night come we got all wet and heavy.

"And when the third day comes Lawrence couldn't walk much longer. His end of his left leg start to get hurt and his stomach and so we got very slow. And that day he is going to left his stuff behind. And so I start to drag his hunting bag for him. Take all the heavy stuff off.

"And that night when my shoulders start feel tired took it off and stop to have little sleep. And fourth day he couldn't walk and he told us to go on to try to get to save place.

"And covered him with little snow, and he tell us to say prayer for him. After we left him and say our prayer for him and we start out again. "We didn't want to left him behind. He told us to go on and start walk as young ice it moving. Very cold day.

"And on the fifth day I start to feel my left foot freeze and so does Raphael start to feel his feet too and his hands. And no longer he couldn't keep up with me.

"And finally he couldn't even stand up. I let try three times. he said he couldn't make it and start to cry. Told me to go. He said he will pray for me to get to save place.

Only son

Gregory Ayac

"P.S. Please excuse my very poor writing. I will talk again when I get a little stronger. I am so weak right now I couldn't even think some words. I was plenty happy Arnold Olanna find me.

G.A."[16]

What was it that kept Ayac going against seemingly insurmountable odds? His youth, his determination, but especially his faith. "I never did give up hope that I would be safe," he said. "Never lost hope that I would have strength. I believed my prayers and the prayers of Lawrence and Raphael would see me through."[17]

Completely exhausted, with both feet frozen, he received emergency treatment in Nome, and was then flown to the Alaska Native Service Hospital in Kotzebue, where the dead parts of his feet were amputated. He recovered from his incredible journey, but his days as a hunter were over. He moved to Nome, where he worked as a longshoreman and as an ivory carver for 28 years. Tragically — and ironically — his life of 54 years came to an end on 2 September 1977, when he was run down by a hit-and-run driver on a Nome street. The bodies of his two hunting companions were never found.

Excitement ran high on King Island on 7 February 1949, when the icebreaker *U.S.S. Burton Island*, which was in the area to observe ice movements, tied up to the ice about 150 feet off the island. Natives swarmed aboard and sold, or traded off, goodly quantities of ivory and ivory carvings to crew members. The following day Cunningham said Mass on board. Out of a crew of 145 about 40 attended.[18]

One month later Cunningham wrote to Small, "The captain [Jack E. Gibson] tells me he was making a study of Bering Sea ice and I am in favour of his continuing those studies every winter. He paid me the great compliment of saying he came especially to King Island to see me. I am invited to accompany them on a three weeks' or month's trip east of Point Barrow this coming summer. I have written Bishop Gleeson for permission, if it is convenient for me to make the trip when the Navy is ready, which is doubtful. I have always had the ambition to begin a mission along the arctic coast east of Barrow, and this is an excellent opportunity to look the population over, try out the language, etc."[19]

That Gibson, the captain of the *Burton Island*, was favorably impressed by Cunningham, the first person he met at King Island, is evident
from his remarks in an address to the St. Paul's Methodist Men's and
Women's Clubs in Newport, Rhode Island, almost eight years later:
"Father Tom is probably the best known and best loved missionary in
Alaska, not particularly because of his Catholic religion, and not because
of the many years of his life he has spent in Little Diomede, King Island,
and Barrow village, but rather because he is the very fine man that he is."[20]

"I am not Catholic," Gibson later wrote to George T. Boileau, S.J.,
"but Father Tom's sincere, warm personality attracted me immediately
as it must have attracted so many thousands whom he helped in his
life. His philosophy, the deep admiration and love of the Ukivok Eskimos
for him, and his exceedingly small, plain, cold lodgings, warmed by
his personality, left a deep and lasting impression on me."[21] For the
rest of his life Gibson treasured a sealskin rifle scabbard and a copy
of the *Phonetic Guide* Cunningham had given him when he visited King
Island.

A footnote to Alaska bush aviation was written on St. Patrick's Day,
1949, when Tex Ziegler, from Marys Igloo, became the first pilot to
land on top of King Island. He came because Cunningham wanted to
go to Diomede. The next day all the King Islanders went to Mass and
Communion, and then to the top of the island to see Ziegler and Cunningham take off at 11:00 a.m. "The operation was hazardous," Cunningham noted in the diary.

He stayed a week in Nome, making the acquaintance of the new
pastor, Neil K. Murphy, S.J., and visiting with Oregon Province Provincial Small. The last week of March and the first week of April he spent
in Teller, and on 6 April he went to Diomede, where the congregation
seemed pleased to have him come. The Diomede population was at this
time down to 99 from the 140 it had been when he first went there
in 1936. "Our neighbours on the other island have been very quiet all
winter," he wrote in the diary. "None of the natives have come across,
nor have ours dared go over."[22]

He followed his customary routine on Diomede. His presence was
appreciated, and religious services and catechism classes were well attended. He had hoped to have a long stay there that spring, but so
anxious were the King Islanders to have him back on their island that
they sent two skinboats, with 28 men aboard, to retrieve him. They
arrived on 5 June, but "terrible weather, the sea covered with ice, low

intermittent fog, and a gale blowing from the S.W." kept them weather-
bound at Diomede. They began to worry. On the 8th they asked Cunningham to contact the Coast Guard icebreaker *Northwind* in hopes that
it would transport them home to their island. Contact was made, and
the next day the *Northwind* took them and Cunningham to King Island.

During the months of July, August, and September, 1949, Cunningham
— who had been in the Army Officers' Reserve Corps since October
1946 — was on active duty, stationed at Marks Air Force Base in Nome.
He made several trips to Fort Richardson near Anchorage, to Kotzebue,
and one to Juneau. Army headquarters were so appreciative of his services that they informed him that henceforth he would be able to write
his own ticket as regards active duty. While on active duty, Cunningham
was, nevertheless, "able to keep in close contact with the islanders, who
behaved very well."[23]

The Bureau of Indian Affairs ship, the *North Star*, returned the King
Islanders and Cunningham to the island on 2 October for what was
to be his last winter there. With him he brought lumber to repair the
church and a two and a half kilowatt generator to provide power for
the lights in his house and the church, and for some "street" lights.

The October and November King Island diary entries seem to have
been made by a doctor rather than by a missionary priest. An epidemic
of measles swept the village and brought down all the smaller children.
Measles were followed by colds. Several babies were born; several infants
died. Mothers were sick. Cunningham himself was incapacitated for a
time with what he thought was a cracked rib — "hurt on the edge
of an oil barrel." On 28 November he "performed a minor operation
on the schoolteacher's thumbnail."

Asked once what he would do if he himself needed medical attention
while on Diomede, he answered, "Take care of myself — I had to once.
I smashed my finger during a trip to Nome, and the doctor sewed it
up. When I came back to Diomede, I hurt it and tore it open again.
I couldn't go back to Nome, so I froze my finger until it became numb,
[then] sewed it up with seal sinew."[24]

The "Fighting Irish" of Notre Dame, by finishing the 1949 football
season undefeated and untied, found a place in the King Island diary
under date of 4 December. Cunningham knew the team's record from
his radio. During his Diomede years, having no radio, he had "heard
no news, good or bad, sacred or profane," for at that time he considered
a radio a luxury he could not afford. Furthermore, he claimed that

he got along well enough without one. He did, however, admit, "I would like the football scores and the boxing news, but what's the difference anyhow."[25] By December 1949, on remote King Island, he not only learned the scores, but was able to follow the Notre Dame games, play by play.

On 1 January 1950, Cunningham wrote in the diary, "A nice, mild day ushered in the new year," a new year that was to usher in significant changes in his life. On 17 February he received a wire informing him that he had been transferred from the Army Officers' Reserve Corps to the Air Force Reserve — same rank and same time in grade, a transfer he had requested in September the previous year, giving as reasons his location and a belief that his services could be used more readily in the Air Force than in the Army.[26]

On the feast of his patron saint, he wrote to the editor of the *Jesuit Yearbook* in Melbourne, Australia: "St. Patrick is not feeling kindly towards the Irish today. It's the worst day of winter, which withal has been unseasonably mild. The wind NE is over 75 mph. That's as high as my recorder goes. It's 14 degrees below zero and blowing snow. Since morning the gale has torn off the stove pipe from the church and house. I had to tie myself to the roof to replace the one on the house. One guy-wire of the windcharger snapped, which leaves my generator and tower lying on a slope and being quickly covered with snow. A strong current is piling up enormous pressure ridges of ice along the rocks and the shore of the island. The only favourable item is that there is beginning to be a reasonable amount of daylight, and the day is too stormy for the children to come to a catechism class, so I can skip four ¾-hour periods of instruction with a clear conscience. But there were over 50 people at Mass this morning out of a population of 160."

Cunningham, scheduled to go on short-term active duty in the Air Force Reserve at Marks Air Force Base the next day, left King Island for the last time in his own boat on 30 June 1950.[27]

10 / U.S. Air Force Chaplain: 1950-1952

Cunningham underwent a physical examination on 25 July 1950, after which he certified himself to be "sound and well and physically qualified for military service." At first he intended to put in only the normal 60 days that he owed as a reservist. However, the U.S. Air Force wanted more than this — and, it seems, so did Cunningham. Again, a series of letters was exchanged among top-ranking military officials, Fitzgerald's successor Bishop Francis D. Gleeson, S.J., Oregon Province Provincial Small, and Cunningham.

Cunningham spent most of the summer of 1950 in and around Nome. Several times, however, he was ordered to Fort Richardson for one- and two-week periods of "chaplain activities" with the Alaskan Air Command. Cunningham wanted his Superiors to believe that the military was putting pressure on him to commit himself to a regular tour of active duty. This the military was certainly doing — and with little or no opposition from Cunningham, a maneuver that was not lost on Small, a wise and perceptive man, who wrote Gleeson on 19 October, "I fear that Fr. Tom himself is angling to get into the service." Small, moreover, had other plans for Cunningham at this time. He wanted him to "go up to Barrow and try to establish a foothold in that part of the world," which Cunningham was to do — as we shall see below — but not for several more years.

Gleeson, however, sided with the military and Cunningham, and wrote to Small on 21 October, "Fr. Cunningham's case is settled. Day before yesterday the head of chaplains in Alaska called me from Anchorage and urged me to withdraw the time limit and send immediate approval of Fr. Cunningham's return to active duty. The 21st was supposed to be a kind of deadline in the matter, as it was the end of the three months' summer stretch. Thinking you would most likely approve, I sent wires to the Military Ordinariate and to the head of Air Force chaplains in Wash. D.C. withdrawing the one year condition." So, Cunningham was again on a prolonged tour of active duty — from 30 October 1950 to 29 July 1952, this time with the U.S. Air Force.

What the service seems to have wanted from Cunningham was not only his priestly "chaplain activities," but especially his expertise in arctic ice conditions. Cunningham was a recognized expert on pack ice and arctic survival, and served the Air Force in an advisory capacity after reporting to the 19th Air Rescue Squadron headquartered at Elmendorf Air Force Base. (On 21 November, he was transferred to the Air Force's 5005th hospital, also at Elmendorf.)

As an arctic advisor, Cunningham received all official bulletins relating to a unique experimental weather station that was planned for the polar ice pack, especially since he was to be a key figure in the project, although a volunteer. In June, 1950, the Alaskan Air Command issued a bulletin, which read in part: "The possibility of increased air traffic over the Arctic Ocean requires a thorough knowledge of weather conditions and communications problems peculiar to polar flying operations. Info concerning the logistical support of a manned weather station on the polar ice pack and the capabilities and limitations of rescue operations is essential for successful air operations in this area... This command will establish an experimental base on the polar ice pack approx. 200 miles north of Barter Island prior to 15 Aug. '50 to obtain info concerning weather and communication problems, the feasibility of logistical support for such a station, and the capabilities and limitations of rescue operations in the polar regions." The communique also went on to say that only "hand-picked volunteers" were to serve at the experimental station, and for only two-week periods. (It was supposed, apparently, that the Arctic— that pitiless, howling desert of ice and snow, of midnight sun, of noonday darkness, of seasons of long shadows — could be endured for only a short time even by hand-picked volunteers.)

Cunningham himself apparently suggested a postponement of the experiment until early 1951, for he received a bulletin from the 10th Air Rescue Squadron, dated 12 December 1950, that "permission was received from Alaskan Air Command to postpone establishment of experimental base on polar ice pack until on or about 1 February 1951."

While waiting to go, Cunningham was frequently called away from his primary assignment as chaplain at the USAF hospital at Elmendorf to give lectures on arctic survival at various Arctic Indoctrination Schools. In mid-January, 1951, he was ordered to spend "two days at Army Indoctrination School [at Big Delta] to conduct chaplain activities," and soon thereafter, seven days on St. Lawrence Island for the same purpose. On both occasions he unquestionably conducted "chaplain activities," but the primary purpose of such trips was, beyond doubt, to teach arctic survival courses.

When Cunningham received his special orders in February to proceed to Barter Island, he was scheduled to be there for approximately 30 days, despite the "two-week" stay announced by the bulletin of June, 1950. Cunningham must have embraced this volunteer assignment with enthusiasm, for on Barter Island he would again be in his native element, on an island surrounded by water and ice. Moreover, he had for years been wanting to explore the arctic coast with a view to establishing Catholic missions there, and this would afford him an opportunity to do so.

On 14 February, he wrote to friends John and Gerry Gaughan, "It's 8:30 p.m., 40° below zero, 25-mph wind, and no prospects of going anywhere tonight." (Cunningham and John P. Gaughan first met in 1948 when Gaughan, an Air Force officer, was stationed in Nome. They became fast friends. Several years later when the two served together at Elmendorf, Cunningham met Gaughan's wife, Gerry, and the children. The Gaughan-Cunningham friendship was a close one, generated many letters, and lasted until the latter's death.)

Cunningham and the "Polar Ice Pack" crew arrived on Barter Island the first week in February and immediately found bad weather. While waiting for a break in the weather — which was "blowing the mother and father of all blizzards" — Cunningham scouted out the Eskimo settlement on the island. "I can converse easily enough with the local Natives," he wrote, "and they seemed surprised to find military personnel speaking Eskimo."

Every morning at 7:00 he held Mass, at which four of the five Catholics in his party of eight were daily communicants — "which makes everything so much better," he wrote, "and we have the grace of God on our side." In the evenings he played Ping-Pong, at which he could beat everybody there. "Not much of an accomplishment," he admitted, "but still a minor distinction."

When the weather improved, on 20 February, he and Captain Marion F. Brinegar flew out over the polar ice cap to find a suitable floe on which to set up the proposed experimental base. Roughly 200 miles north of Barter Island they found what they were looking for, and camp "Polar Ice Pack," consisting of three 16' × 16' hastily erected prefabricated Jamesway huts, was established the same day with Brinegar and Cunningham in charge of the eight-man project.[1]

From this arctic oasis Cunningham wrote to the Gaughans again, "We now have the camp in full-scale operation, and are probably finding out things that might be useful to somebody some day. My special job is safety, which means scouting around the area a distance of 3 to 5 miles per day, and trying to ascertain from the cracks in the ice just when we will have to pack up and leave in a hurry. A lot of this is pure malarky, of course, but it does the men good, when I come home and say we are safe for another 48 hours."[2]

Father Tom in early 1951 offering Mass on an altar of carved snow blocks on the polar ice cap north of Barter Island. Members of the 10th Air Rescue Squadron attended. *(U.S. Air Force photo. Oregon Province Archives)*

For 17 days everything at the polar ice pack camp went pretty well as anticipated. Cunningham, whose duty it was to monitor ice conditions daily, knew, however, that the camp was on anything but *terra firma*, and that its days were numbered from the very outset of its establishment. "We are convinced we are here to stay," wrote Cunningham on 3 March; and, on the following day, "We are on good ice for some time yet." However, on the 10th, a 150-foot-wide crack opened up about one hundred feet to the east of the camp. The following day there was major ice movement right near the camp. By 6:30 a.m. on the 12th it was obvious that the camp would have to be abandoned, "so we moved all movable equipment out of Jamesway huts on the solid ice in back of us. There was no immediate danger, but, for the sake of safety of all the men, we called Barter Island and asked them to send us a plane as early as they could, because it seemed likely that we would be abandoning camp. The plane came in midday. In the meantime the ice had kept on coming, and eventually twisted two Jamesway huts into the pressure ridge. We had to walk approximately one mile from the camp over the pressure ridge, which was continuing to build up, to where the plane landed. They had landed on the strip that they used all the time, but it had drifted away considerable distance. During the evacuation of the camp, there was no danger as all movements of the ice could be anticipated. The morning was very cold — 35 degrees below zero, and the wind about 18 miles an hour."[3] When on the 15th, 16th, and 17th of March flights were made out to the area where the camp had been, no trace of it could be found.

For the most part, life on the floe had been bleak and monotonous. Extremely low temperatures — down to minus 55 degrees — and unrelenting blizzards seemed to be the order of the day. And yet, boreal nature knew how to vary its routine and to compensate those who had come to challenge it. "When the wind goes down," Cunningham wrote, "it is very, very silent — at times frighteningly so. You listen in vain for a dog howling or a jeep chugging along the road." And to relieve the monochromatic sameness of snow-covered ice, there were the multicolored splendors of the arctic sky. "Almost nightly," he wrote to the Gaughans, "we have wonderful displays of northern lights. Sunday night there was a rainbow-like trail over the whole sky. The colors were twisting and changing like an enormous skein of yarn. Every clear night there is a great display." (The northern lights here in question must have been extraordinary, for another time Cunningham wrote to the Gaughans, "There has to be a real good display to arouse the poet in me."[4])

This is one of the few passages in Cunningham's writings that might lead one to believe that he had anything like a developed aesthetic sense, that he had eyes and ears for art and beauty. He admitted he found the Eskimo women's bench dance "very beautiful to watch," and in his King Island diary he commented from time to time on the beauty of the singing and the nice altar decorations in the church, but that was about the extent of it. When he had no radio, it was football scores and boxing results that he missed rather than drama, classical music, or opera, in which his taste seems to have been confined exclusively to the music of Gilbert and Sullivan — of which, however, he was very fond.[5]

No sooner was Cunningham back at Elmendorf after his first sojourn on the polar ice cap, than he was airborne again — this time "in connection with chaplain activities and to render religious services" on St. Lawrence Island, in Nome, Kotzebue, Galena, and Ladd Air Force Base near Fairbanks. When he returned from this trip, he found waiting for him a "Letter of Appreciation," dated 17 April 1951, from the commanding officer of the Army Arctic Indoctrination School at Big Delta. From this we learn that, on 18 January, Cunningham had given a conference on "Eskimo Life" which provided his audience with "a keen insight into life in the Far North," and was "unique for its color and human interest." He had spoken with "an authority that evoked the admiration of the entire student body."

(This was not the first time that Cunningham's services, both as chaplain and Arctic expert, were appreciated, for Frank A. Armstrong, Jr., Major General, U.S. Air Force, had written him earlier, on 23 December 1950, that it was his "pleasure to extend my sincere appreciation for the worthwhile services you have rendered this command while on active duty as a chaplain and also while a Jesuit missionary in Alaska. Your outstanding professional ability gained by long personal experience while doing missionary work with the Natives on King Island and Little Diomede has been of great value to this command. You have assisted by rendering information on how to exist in the Arctic, which has been published and put into practice at our Arctic Indoctrination Schools. This and other information that you have been able to furnish this command has proven to be of untold value.")

Cunningham obviously enjoyed a lecturer's role, no matter how small his audience, for Llorente wrote, "The minute he entered a room with people, he filled the room with his presence and began to 'take over.' Nobody resented it; on the contrary, all were pleased to be in his company. Somehow he gave the impression that he was speaking with authority."[6]

In June Cunningham was ordered to the USAF School of Aviation
Medicine at Randolph Field, Texas, and to Gunter and Maxwell Air
Force Bases in Alabama to lecture on "Life and Survival in the Arctic."
So impressed was the acting commandant of Randolph Field with Cunn-
ingham's lecture that he wrote a "Letter of Appreciation" to the com-
manding general of the Alaskan Air Command expressing his "sincere
appreciation for the excellent address presented by Chaplain Cunningham."
Major General John D. Barker, deputy commanding general of Maxwell
AFB, likewise expressed his appreciation to the head of the Alaskan Air
Command for Cunningham's generous services.

One could easily get the impression that Cunningham's tour of active
duty as a chaplain was one long, uninterrupted round of high adventure,
of hobnobbing with top military brass, of honors. True, his 21 months
in the U.S. Air Force were anything but commonplace or monotonous.
And he did move easily and often among top ranking officers who appreciated his services and gave him tangible evidence of their appreciation. Still, numerous papers and letters in his archive file attest to the
fact that he always attended painstakingly to ordinary, routine chaplain
business, that he was always ready to help those in need, that he had
time for all, especially the "underdog." "Whenever anyone was in trouble or needed help," wrote one who knew him at this time, "Father
Tom had a way of just happening along."[7]

Enlisted men regularly asked him to write letters on their behalf to
their commanding officers — letters requesting, for example, "emergency
leave for soldier whose mother is ill and has very little means of support,"
or "leave for enlisted man to be present for the birth of his first child."
Through his intercession others sought "compassionate change of status,"
"hardship discharge, being the sole support of his mother and grand-
father," "morale leave," and the like. Captain Cunningham, military
chaplain though he was, remained at the same time and always the
simple, approachable priest, Father Tom.

Although he was by temperament clearly an extrovert, he had, nevertheless, a deep spiritual side to him — and it was this that made him
so effective when dealing with people and their personal problems. "I
was told by the head chaplain in Anchorage [Colonel William J. Clasby],"
wrote Alaska Mission Superior Norman E. Donohue, S.J., after Cunningham was separated from the Air Force, "that Fr. Cunningham was
considered a saint in the service, because he rose daily at 4:00 a.m.
and made an hour of prayers every morning before Mass. Many young

men were converted or returned to the faith through his instructions."[8]
In the spring of 1951, Cunningham and Captain John M. Geary,
a biologist, sat down together in the Ladd AFB Officers Club and discussed
"the problem of digging up the Eskimos at Nome." The idea — very
likely it came from Cunningham — was to disinter some of the 200
Eskimos who were buried in a mass grave after the influenza epidemic
of 1918-19 in hopes of finding bodies and the virus, which caused the
epidemic, in a refrigerated state and thus gain valuable medical
knowledge.[9] Virologists from Harvard, Yale, and Michigan medical schools
were to take part in the project. On 19 July, Cunningham from Elmendorf and members of the Arctic Aeromedical Laboratory from Ladd
met in Nome to dig up the Eskimos. As far as can be determined the
cooperation of the Eskimo Council in Nome and the permission of the
Nome District Court had been obtained in advance, but, for reasons
unknown, the project was never carried through.[10]

On 26 November 1951, Cunningham was appointed one of the four
consultors to the General Superior of the Alaska Mission. This meant
that he had to attend meetings convened several times a year by the
Mission Superior and to express his views as to what he thought good
for the Alaska Mission. He served as a consultor to the end of his life.

During the last quarter of 1951 and the first quarter of 1952, Cunningham continued to travel much of the time to conduct religious services
and to give character guidance and survival lectures at military bases
scattered throughout Alaska: St. Lawrence Island, Nome, Tin City,
Kotzebue, Cape Lisburne, Big Delta, Ladd, Naknek, and all the way
to Shemya near the end of the Aleutian chain.

By mid-March 1952, he was back at the Elmendorf hospital — now
not only as chaplain, but as a patient. He was admitted, according
to his "Clinical Record," on 15 March, "following severe over-work and
lack of rest for many months. Diagnosis: bronchial pneumonia." Twenty
days later, on 3 April, he was discharged, and on the seventh, he went
to Mt. McKinley Rest and Recreation Center for 15 days — not, however,
for rest and recreation, but "for purpose of conducting religious services
and character guidance lectures."

Cunningham began his 30-day annual leave in the third week of June,
the first part of which he spent on a trip to the east coast. While there
he was invited to a banquet hosted by Archbishop Cushing of Boston.
At the banquet he completely shattered clerical protocol — caused a
mild sensation — when he pushed the main course, boiled lobster, aside,

and insisted instead on a plate of ham and eggs, protesting that, after nearly two decades in Alaska, the latter was the real delicacy.[11]

Cunningham next flew to Denver to visit friends he had made in Alaska, the Gaughans and Major Ranger Curran and his family, with whom he stayed as a house guest. Shortly after his visit to Denver, the *Denver Register* carried a feature article about him, which did much to enhance the Cunningham legend. The author of the article, Ed Mack Miller, found Cunningham "a very humble man...after all, only a priest." But from Cunningham's admiring friends he learned, too, that "the modest priest, who would volunteer little news about himself," was "one of the world's most fabulous priests...recognized as the United States' outstanding authority on operations above the Arctic Circle," a man who, "on nine separate occasions, while on duty as an advisor to the Air Force...made parachute jumps alone into the wastes of the Arctic to aid lost parties. One group he brought back was the crew of a Russian plane." (He also wrote that Cunningham was "a seasoned pilot, at ease at the controls of a plane high above the frozen tundra.")

In an article entitled "Adventure is his parish," Miller wrote, "Once, shortly after World War II, [Cunningham] came close to cashing in his frosty chips. He went seal-hunting with an Eskimo foursome on the ice cap off King Island. Each man took out for himself, crawling over the ice toward the open sea. Close to the edge Father Tom's particular resting place suddenly cracked free of the pack and he found himself on an ice raft floating in the Bering Sea — toward Siberia.

"As the weather worsened and the temperature plummeted, he kept himself alive by alternated hard exercise (taken in the nude in temperatures in the vicinity of 40 below zero so that perspiration would not freeze inside his clothes) with brief catnaps. For four days he floated in a gray ocean of screaming cold. He was able to kill a seal, fortunately, which gave him plenty of food. Finally, he floated back to near where he had begun, and a hard journey on foot brought him back to the Eskimo tribe."[12]

Cunningham was, obviously, good copy, and the press knew well how to get a great deal of highly readable journalistic mileage out of him and his doings. However, some of the things written about him — the passages just cited from Miller's pieces, for instance — were merely fanciful fabrications with shreds of truth woven in here and there.

Parachute jumping would, to be sure, have been wholly in keeping with Cunningham's character and lifestyle, and the circumstances under

which he supposedly made the jumps — while with the Nome-based
Search and Rescue Squadron — make Miller's account of the jumps
sound entirely plausible. Other materials in Cunningham's archive file
also contain references to his parachuting.[13] However, Anable and
Gaughan, who were with him in Nome during the period of the alleged
jumps, know nothing of them. Anable, a reliable witness, is strongly
inclined to doubt any such ever took place.[14]

According to what Cunningham himself wrote in a letter to Louis
L. Renner, S.J., he *was* lost once on the ice for three days,[15] but that
he had kept himself from freezing to death by exercising in the nude
at 40 degrees below zero becomes believable only at the same price
grand opera is believable — the willing suspension of disbelief.

There is no evidence to support the claim that Cunningham was ever
a licensed pilot. The evidence points rather to the contrary. Gaughan
wrote of him, "He was not a pilot himself, but enjoyed flying and was
always happy on the frequent flights on which he went with me to
get a chance to take the controls."[16]

Cunningham as expert parachutist, Cunningham as nude exerciser at
minus 40, Cunningham as seasoned pilot: all are authentic parts of Cunningham as legend — a legend fostered in part by a press inclined toward
sensationalism, in part by his admiring, too-credulous friends, and in
part by Cunningham himself. " 'He's a legend, all right!' admitted Father
[George E.] Carroll, [S.J.], 'and he helps it along.' "[17] Already during
his lifetime, there was a legendary dimension to the man Cunningham;
but this dimension, too, has to be looked upon as a real, authentic part
of him. Without it the Cunningham portrait would not be complete.

As Cunningham's tour of active duty in the Air Force was drawing
to a close, there was a movement afoot in higher military echelons to
persuade him to extend his time of active service. But he wanted out,
and asked Major General William D. Old, commanding officer at Elmendorf, not to approve the extension. He promised, however, to go on
active duty occasionally for special assignments. Old sided with Cunningham, and on 29 July 1952 he received payment for 30 days of unused
accrued leave, and reverted to inactive status in the Air Force Reserve.[18]

"Looking back on the two years of service," Cunningham wrote to
the Gaughans, "I think it was well worth it. I made some wonderful
friends, and I certainly learned plenty myself. The night before I left
the hospital, all 44 nurses gave me a very fancy dinner, and presented
me with 250 dollars towards building my new church north of the Brooks

Range. Chapel #2 really went to town and gave me a gift of $1600 for the same purpose. Fr. Clasby preached at all the Masses and, you know him. He had the people weeping. Besides liking me personally, Fr. C. has a genuine admiration for any priest who works in Northern Alaska."[19]

11 / Kotzebue: 1952-1954

Although Cunningham's effective date of separation from the U.S. Air Force was 29 July 1952, he was kept on till the end of August to do "jobs the [Alaskan Air] Command had been getting around for two years to ask...to go around on a trip to all the radar sites."[1]

He spent September and October helping out in the Fairbanks parish. General Old, on 30 September, fired off one last round of appreciation to Cunningham: "...my appreciation for the outstanding services performed by you in the past two years...numerous favorable comments

St. Francis Xavier Church in Kotzebue as it appeared during Father Tom's time there.
(Alaskan Shepherd collection)

on the excellent presentation and interesting content of your lectures...The exceptional results you obtained despite limited facilities, severe weather and difficult transportation make your achievements all the more significant."

On 5 November, in an Air Force plane, Cunningham — who had

felt himself drawn to missionary work in the Arctic ever since he came to Alaska as a priest — was flown to Kotzebue for the winter 1952-53. On board with him was his recently purchased team of seven dogs, along with sled and harnesses. Kotzebue had been without a resident pastor since the previous year, when Father George E. Carroll left to become the pastor of King Island.[2]

Cunningham anticipated that his winter at Kotzebue, his first beyond the Arctic Circle, would be a time for making long-range preparations for his projected new field of missionary work along the arctic coast. After writing to the Gaughans about "shipping lumber, etc." north, he continued, "I am not too enthusiastic about the new project, or rather Tom C. isn't, but Father Tom C., S.J., is."[3]

Although Cunningham was officially stationed at Kotzebue during the winter of 1952-1953, he was away much of the time. Early in January 1953, he was called to Nome because of his ability to speak French. The Little Sisters of Jesus, of French origin, who had established themselves in Nome only the previous August and were unable to converse well in English, especially about spiritual matters, had asked him to hear their confessions and to provide them with spiritual guidance in their own language. In February, he spent six days on Little Diomede because a flu epidemic, in which six people died, was ravaging the village.[4] In early April he again visited Diomede for a short time, and from 15 April to the 27th, he was in Barrow making further preparations for the establishment of a mission in the high Arctic.

From Barrow he wrote the Gaughans, "Am now arranging the preliminaries for putting up two buildings in the vicinity, one here and the other near the mouth of the Colville River. This should be my last project. I can take all the sympathy you want to hand out until about Sept. 1955. After that I should be comfortable, and will put my feet on the kitchen table, read a book and relax. A good part of next winter I will probably spend wandering around with the nomadic tribe, and live in a tent which is a prospect I don't anticipate with any great pleasure. But the results will be worth it."[5]

Before returning to Kotzebue, Cunningham gave talks on Eskimo life and arctic survival at Ladd AFB and Big Delta Army Base at the end of April, and on 15 May, he was back on Diomede again, to spend six weeks there, mostly in catechizing and instructing his somewhat neglected flock. Response was good, even though it was somewhat late in the season for indoor activity. In June he put brick-finish tarpaper on the two exposed sides of the church and painted the woodwork and window frames.

On 10 June 1953, Cunningham received his appointment as an ecclesiastical, auxiliary chaplain of the Military Ordinariate for all U.S. military establishments at Cape Lisburne, Barrow, Barter Island, Umiat, Anaktuvuk Pass, and any other military bases north of the Brooks Range. With this appointment he was constituted military pastor of the Arctic. He was already officially the missionary pastor of that region.

During the first part of July he spent time at Barrow and Barter Island, returning to Kotzebue on the 14th. There he became sick—"collapsed a couple of times" — and in early August went to Fairbanks for treatment. According to the Fairbanks diary, his problem was diagnosed as high blood pressure brought on apparently by some heavy drinking.[6] After treatment he was able to spend the latter part of August in Barrow, and though he continued to make his headquarters in Kotzebue, he was able to make periodic trips to the arctic coast during the last three months of 1953.

During the first quarter of 1954, Cunningham again ranged widely throughout much of Alaska. Bethel, Nome, Galena, Umiat, Point Hope, Cape Lisburne, Kotzebue, Big Delta, Nenana, Teller, Lost River, Marys Igloo, Barrow all saw his coming and going. "The church in Point Barrow is practically finished," he wrote the Gaughans on 26 March, "and I have had close contact with the wandering Eskimos." He also wrote, "In a few days I will go over to Diomede Island until the ice goes out...Possibly I will spend a couple of months on Diomede every year, as it's my first church and first love." It must have been consoling for him to be able to write in the Diomede diary on 18 April, "Easter Sunday: 100% turned out this morning, all capable of so doing receiving Holy Communion. Six children made their first Communion. The choir was excellent."

Anticipating a visit by Bishop Gleeson, who was to come and confirm all those eligible, Cunningham taught three catechism classes daily, "well attended." For the first time on Diomede, he taught catechism and prayers in both Eskimo and English in anticipation of any non-Eskimo speaking priest who might succeed him on the island.

Around 11:00 a.m., on 2 May 1954, Gleeson landed on the ice at the foot of the island. This was the first time ever that a major Superior of any kind had set foot on Diomede, and it was a great occasion for the islanders. Thirty people were confirmed in an impressive ceremony.

The singing was excellent. Thirteen children made their first Holy Communion. Six National Guardsmen from Diomede were the guard of honor all through the ceremony.[7]

When Cunningham left a week later for Nome, Fairbanks, and points north, he was never to see Little Diomede again, but he left it with his missionary work, begun 18 years earlier, very well done.

12 / Barrow, DEWline, Ice Skate: 1954-1958

"I am on a little job for the AF for the moment," wrote Cunningham to the Gaughans on 16 May 1954. "Right now I am at a spot designated as NAE, and it's along the Canadian arctic coast, east of the dividing line. It's a joint US-Can. project and everyone is a scientist of some kind. The only way I can shine is by being able to speak Eskimo to the lone Eskimo family in 250 miles of coast line. This job will terminate in two weeks, and then I will continue on at Point Barrow. The work there is progressing nicely, and from now on I will be able to spend more time there. Eventually, by putting out lots of effort and determination, I should be able to introduce Catholicism north of the Brooks Range, which is the reason I came to Alaska in the first place."

It will be remembered that 18 years earlier, during his first year in Nome, Cunningham had written to Crimont on 26 February 1936 about the Church's establishing itself at Wainwright and Barrow, but it was not until 16 June 1954 that the pastor in Fairbanks could write in the house diary, "Fr. Cunningham left for Barrow. He will begin his permanent missionary work there."

The idea of establishing Catholic missions along the arctic coast was by no means a new one. As early as the summer of 1898 Jesuit Father Francis A. Barnum had sailed north on the revenue steamer *Bear* to scout out that region. "My object in making this reconnaissance of the arctic coast," he wrote, "was to see what prospects there were for mission work."[1] Owing to a shortage of manpower, nothing was ever done in the high Arctic until Cunningham's arrival in the 1950s. As a Christian missionary to Barrow he was, of course, a latecomer. The Presbyterians had established a mission there in 1890.

Barrow is situated approximately 345 miles above the Arctic Circle on the shores of the Arctic Ocean. In the 1950s this northernmost United States community was mostly a jumble of wood and tarpaper houses and shacks scattered at random along the edge of the polar sea. Its population numbered just over a thousand, mostly Eskimos, all of whom had by this time either accepted or rejected Christianity.

A rather diverse ministry faced Cunningham when he took up station in Barrow. There were the white Catholics in Barrow itself: construction workers, military personnel, people connected with the school, the hospital, the U.S. Weather Bureau, and the Civil Aeronautics Administration. Soon he was to minister also to the men working at the Distant Early Warning System radar sites, the DEWline, located at regular intervals to the west and to the east all the way into Canada. Moreover, in those pre-ecumenical days, he was expected to, and hoped to, make converts even among the Christian Eskimos in Barrow and outlying villages. Officially his parish consisted of the whole Alaskan Arctic — everything north of the Arctic Circle except Kotzebue.

To cover his vast arctic parish of 150,000 square and frozen miles, the largest Catholic parish under the U.S. flag, Cunningham planned to travel by dog team and on military planes. He was still in the Air Force Reserve at this time, and enjoyed the privilege of being authorized by the commander of the Alaskan Air Command to travel on any military aircraft on a space available basis.[2]

During the summer of 1954, while living in an old rented Eskimo house, Cunningham was preoccupied with getting his mission complex in Barrow built, preferably from surplus military material. He had written the year before to the Gaughans, "When the Navy begins raining down the duck-soup, I want to be there with a fork,"[3] for he planned to build his church, not from the tundra up with new materials, but on pilings, and out of a surplus quonset hut located four miles from Barrow, and from lumber salvaged from the abandoned Umiat Air Force Base.

The Air Force flew the lumber to Barrow free of charge. Cunningham and two hired Eskimos, helped by volunteers from the Air Force, from the white community, and from the Puget Sound and Drake construction camp, cut the 20' × 56' steel quonset in half and moved it to the church site with a D-4 tractor and sledges borrowed from the Weather Bureau.[4]

While construction was going on, the weather was none too cooperative. The temperature stayed below the freezing mark for a week in mid-July.

The wind that blew off the pack ice crowding the shore made building conditions "altogether cold and miserable." Once Cunningham commented, "The Arctic has no warm weather; just different kinds of cold."

St. Patrick's Church in Barrow, 1958. Father Tom is standing on the right. *(Photo credit: THE AIRMAN Magazine. Alaskan Shepherd collection)*

Nevertheless, despite inclement weather, he was able to write to the Gaughans on 28 July, "The building is well on the way to completion," and on 16 August, "The people are enthusiastic about St. Patrick's Church." (As founder and builder of the Barrow mission, Cunningham had the right to name the church as he pleased. He chose to honor his patron saint.) By 1 November the living quarters, 12' × 24', also used as a temporary chapel, were ready for occupancy. While building, Cunningham received a "surprise amount of volunteer labor," but he himself did most of the carpentry work and all of the wiring. That first winter his quarters were very cold because of a shortage of insulation material. The one oil-burning kitchen range had difficulty raising the temperature to fifty degrees.[5]

The church part of the complex was considered completely finished in the summer of 1955, but only after a 350-pound locomotive bell had been hung in the central tower. The bell had been procured specially for Cunningham's church by Colonel John E. Carroll, who had persuaded the president of the Great Northern Railway to donate it. General Patrick Carter arranged to have it flown from Seattle to Barrow, gratis.[6]

Four times during his first year in Barrow, Cunningham lectured at the Army Arctic Indoctrination School at Big Delta.[7] His many lectures on arctic survival and on the Eskimos of northern Alaska had made him known and esteemed to the point where he could write to the Gaughans on 28 July 1954, "I am informed that I am a member of the Alaskan Scientific Institute, whatever that is, and must preside and give talks at the meeting of that body in Anchorage." He immediately set about resigning, but Bishop Gleeson told him to go — which he did. After the meeting, which took place from 7-10 September, Cunningham returned to Barrow via Fairbanks, and the Fairbanks diarist recorded, "He reported that he was given a very favorable hearing in his report on Eskimo customs, morals, etc."

Cunningham was a very careful observer of the ways of the Eskimos he lived and worked with, but he never studied them formally as would an anthropologist. Nor, as far as can be determined, did he ever read much of the scientific literature dealing with them. He was a practical man, who devoted his time to the active apostolate rather than to theoretical science. He himself remarked when discussing the origins of the

Altar alcove of St. Patrick's Church in Barrow, circa 1960. *(Alaskan Shepherd collection)*

Eskimos, "Frankly, I really don't give a darn where they come from. But I'm vitally interested in where they're going to later on."[8]

Father Tom, after making an eight-day retreat at St. Mary's Mission, February 1955, heading for the plane parked in front of the mission on the Andreafsky River. Mission boys and Ursuline Sisters Lucy (fur coat) and Athanasia accompany him. *(Photo by Paul Linssen, S.J. Oregon Province Archives)*

He was essentially a pastor of souls, a missionary. In Barrow, even before his new mission building was finished, he was instructing potential Eskimo converts, claiming in January, 1955, to have as many as sixty under instruction.[9] However, when it came to converting arctic coast Eskimos, including Barrow, he proved to be no great success. Several factors seem to have been largely responsible for his meager results: the long delay he insisted on before prospective converts were received into the Church, the fact that most of the Eskimos in that area had already embraced some form of Christianity, and because he was on the move so much of the time during his Barrow years.[10]

In late April, 1955, General James H. Doolittle came to Barrow for a polar bear hunt. He had success, bagging two. While in Barrow, Doolittle visited Cunningham "quite often, showed himself very friendly and genuinely interested in our work here. He is retiring and unspectacular."[11]

At this time Cunningham was still in the Air Force Reserve. Effective 1 July 1955 he was promoted from the rank of captain to that of major.

Throughout the summer and fall of 1955, he was busy beyond words. As materials on hand and weather allowed, he tried to paint the outside of his church and put in windows. He traveled almost constantly along the arctic coast, mostly to DEWline sites. He made frequent trips to Anchorage and Fairbanks, and attended a Veterans of Foreign Wars meeting in Juneau. On 10 August he wrote to George T. Boileau, pastor of Immaculate Conception parish in Fairbanks, also his Religious Superior and close personal friend, "Tomorrow I have a Mass here, at the flagship, and at the camp. Monday I have Mass on another ship, plus a lecture in the evening to all Navy personnel in the vicinity. Tuesday I have Mass on an icebreaker that is just returning from the east, and a lecture in the evening to about 70 scientists who have been in the locality. This talk is on the fundamentals of the Eskimo language. Wednesday I have the regular weekday Mass at the camp and a character guidance talk to all Army and Air Force men in the vicinity."

Father Tom offering Mass at one of the DEWline radar sites, circa 1956. *(U.S. Air Force photo. Oregon Province Archives)*

Cunningham made the news in late December when a disastrous fire completely destroyed the Alaska Communications System's powerhouse in Barrow. A picture showing him handling a fire hose appeared in various newspapers.

A fleet of ships carrying materials for the DEWline had put into Barrow in August, and rapid progress was made in constructing the DEWline sites. By early 1956 Cunningham had ten of them in his district, stretching from Point Lay in the west to just beyond the Canadian border in the east. "I try to get around [to] them all with a certain regularity," he wrote the Gaughans on 10 January, "and it works out at a month at home and three weeks on the road, spending two days at each place. All the travel is by air." Of an average of 30 men at each site, only about four were practicing Catholics. Still, he considered his DEWline ministry "all worthwhile."

An important message went out to Cunningham on 22 May 1956 from Major General Joseph H. Atkinson, Commander of the Alaskan Air Command: "By direction of Headquarters, USAF, the Alaskan Air Command is determining the feasibility of establishing a semipermanent scientific station on drifting pack ice in the Arctic Ocean. Station would operate as part of international scientific effort in connection with International Geophysical Year. Initial planning must be submitted to Headquarters, USAF, by 15 June 1956."

This project was to be called variously, "Operation Ice Skate," "Project Ice Skate," and "Drift Station Alpha." Atkinson felt that consultation with Cunningham would be of valuable assistance to the planners of this project, and offered to have him flown to Elmendorf, or to have the planners flown to Barrow, whichever Cunningham preferred. He made the trip to Elmendorf in June. To the Gaughans he wrote on 12 October 1956, "They want me to be in charge of the locating and constructing, and remain until the camp is under way. I know I can do the job, provided I am given sufficient leeway. I am promised enough rank to be impressive."

From 80° 30′ N., 148°W., on 6 April 1957, Cunningham wrote to Boileau, "We are progressing slowly on Ice Skate. It's difficult to locate a good chunk [of ice] that I can reasonably guarantee will last over a year. Last week we established a temporary camp 600 miles out, and are working out of here. Yesterday I think I found an ideal place, so by Wednesday we should begin moving in the permanent equipment. We are living in a tent now. The weather is in the − 40s and 20-30 mph wind. A polar bear and two cubs are uncomfortably close...Little by little everyone is coming around to the plans I set up last June at Elmendorf."

Father Tom, Col. Carlos Alden, Brig. Gen. C.F. Necrason, and Maj. Joseph P. Bilotta, commanding officer of Drift Station Alpha, airborne in a C-47 over the polar ice cap, 1957. *(U.S. Air Force photo. Oregon Province Archives)*

When in 1951 Cunningham selected a floe only 200 miles north of the arctic coast as the site for the experimental weather station, he was, from the outset, not at all satisfied with his choice, being convinced that floes so near land break up much sooner than floes 500 or more miles out. At that time, however, he had no choice in the matter since military authorities had stipulated that the floe be only about 200 miles offshore. This time he was satisfied that a much more suitable floe had been chosen.

Although the floe for the location of Ice Skate was selected jointly by Cunningham and Air Force Colonel Joseph O. Fletcher of Arctic Ice Island T-3 fame,[12] the responsibilities for locating an appropriate camp site and setting up the camp, for guaranteeing reasonable safety, for choosing the final personnel, and for making final decisions in all emergencies rested solely with Cunningham.[13]

In late March the two flew north from Barrow in a B-50 bomber to locate "a good chunk" of drifting pack ice for the proposed scientific station.[14] They examined over 150 square miles of that vast polar icescape before they found their floe, a fog-shrouded sheet of ice about two miles in diameter and from ten to 15 feet thick, adrift in the glacial sea approximately 600 miles north of Barrow. They marked it with brilliant dyes so that they could find it again.[15]

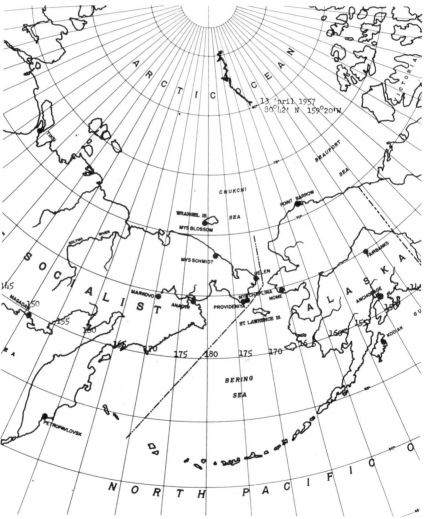

Map shows the location of Drift Station Alpha in April 1957. *(Oregon Province Archives)*

On the days following, flights were made out of Barrow in special long-range, ski-equipped C-47s. As soon as Cunningham and a skeleton work force had landed and set up a temporary camp on 4 April, the Air Force parachuted tractors and other heavy construction equipment to them so that they could scrape, gouge, and blast out a runway for the large C-124 Globemasters to land on.[16]

Airmen in the Jamesway hut kitchen and dining room at Drift Station Alpha, 1957.
(U.S. Air Force photo. Oregon Province Archives)

For a month and a half six of these huge cargo planes made numerous 2800-mile round trips to the site, bringing loads of around 20 tons each on every flight. The permanent camp was intended to house nine civilian scientists and 11 Air Force members, and was expected to last about 18 months. Scientists at the camp were to conduct studies of the Arctic Ocean — its currents, bottom, salinity, temperatures, marine life, and the like.[17]

On Easter Sunday, 21 April 1957, Cunningham had morning Mass at Drift Station Alpha. He then flew the 600 miles south to Barrow for evening Mass. The following day he went north again — on a flight loaded with dynamite, propane gas, and aviation gas. "I think I could accompany an uncrated A-bomb now," he wrote to Boileau on the 23rd. "Our present position," he wrote in that same letter, "is 80° 30'N., 157° 20' W. We move around some, but always in a general good direction. I have been all day dynamiting ice hummocks for the C-124 landing strip. It's a ticklish proposition, because we don't want to blast too deep, but at the same time deep enough. It's a problem. The strip is about half finished now. Tomorrow we expect four Jamesway huts via airdrop, so tomorrow night I can take my sleeping bag off the snow and sleep on a wood floor." On 27 May he was still living in a tent. "I could move to one of the 16' × 16' buildings," he wrote to his brother John, "but I prefer the tent, as I have privacy and have an altar set up in it for Mass in the morning."[18]

Although the drifting station, constructed of prefab, olive-drab Jamesway huts — housing a post office, a mess hall, a recreation hall, living quarters and scientific laboratories — was not completely set up till 5 June, the first scientists arrived around mid-May, and on the 21st the joint U.S. Air Force and International Geophysical Year project was formally opened when Major General James H. Davies, Commander, Alaskan Air Command, planted the American flag on the drifting ice and pronounced the station a "going concern of the United States."[19]

After the ceremony, Davies presented Cunningham and two airmen with the USAF Commendation Ribbon for "meritorious achievement in this most hazardous venture." Davies said to Cunningham, "Father Tom, in utter humility I say this is your field of honor. I commend you for rendering exceptionally meritorious service as a technical advisor on Arctic conditions to the Project Ice Skate Task Group."[20] Speaking of the ribbon, Cunningham wrote to his brother John, "I am quite proud of it, though I must admit, it was earned."

Cunningham felt that the ribbon was well deserved because he had done much more in the establishment of Alpha than merely select a suitable site, which was what the Air Force had initially expected of him. "All that was expected of me," Cunningham wrote to Mark A. Gaffney, S.J., "was to be seated in a tent, or suitable place, and answer questions. But, it didn't work out that way. I am the only one who knew anything about surveying or using a transit. I relieve the cook, took alternate shift when it was necessary to dynamite through pressure ridges, etc."[21]

In an impressive dedication ceremony held at Barrow on 13 August 1957, the Air Force officially accepted the DEWline from the Western Electric Company, the prime contractor for the construction of the line. Participants in the ceremony included various dignitaries, among them several Air Force generals in beribboned uniforms. Sitting with them on the stage was Cunningham, wearing baggy black trousers, a black jacket over his Roman collar, and a beige-colored visor cap. At the close of the ceremony, he gave the benediction.[22]

Father Tom testing the ice near Drift Station Alpha. *(U.S. Air Force photo. Oregon Province Archives)*

In his letter of 27 September 1957 to the Gaughans he speculated about the actual usefulness of the DEWline. "Anyway," he concluded, "you will get your three-hours warning if and when an enemy attacks over the North Pole. I don't think this will ever happen, and the DEWline will never be used. Probably ten years from now the Eskimos will be chasing the lemmings out of the abandoned buildings so they (the Eskimos and possibly myself) can move in."

Drift Station Alpha, May 1957. *(U.S. Air Force photo. Oregon Province Archives)*

With the camp established and operational, Cunningham returned to Barrow to what he described as his "more prosaic job." Nevertheless, he was on call in case of an emergency throughout the whole time Drift Station Alpha was occupied, since he had an agreement with the Air

Father Tom on Drift Station Alpha, 1957, wearing the traditional Eskimo "snow shirt." White color serves the hunter as camouflage. Father Tom is carrying a rifle for protection against polar bears. *(U.S. Air Force photo. Oregon Province Archives)*

Force that he would be there at any sign of danger. Accordingly, the
Air Force had a plane and crew on standby, ready to fly him to the
camp on short notice.[23] He also agreed to spend the darkest and stormiest
time of the year there, so he was on the polar ice cap for three weeks
in October and November. On 6 January 1958 he again flew north
for another three-week stay. "We are in a very stormy period right now,"
he wrote Alaska Mission Superior Henry G. Hargreaves, S.J., on 9 January.
"The temp. has been − 42 to − 58[F.], and the wind up to 48 mph.
We are also bothered by polar bears. They have been roaming around
the camp, tearing up wires and cables, and being a nuisance generally... It's complete and total darkness. My job is safety of the camp,
and the likelihood of our ice floe breaking up, and you judge this possibility
by examining pressure ridges and ice floes five to eight miles away,
and that means a lot of walking. Except when there is a full moon,
I do most of it by ear."

The polar bear was part of what made life at Alpha exciting — and
unpredictable. The previous December a sow and her cub wandered
across the runway just as a C-124 was on final approach. The two knocked over the runway lights and put the whole system out, causing some
confusion. "None of this would happen," wrote Cunningham, "if polar
bears didn't shuffle and drag their feet when walking."[24]

From 3 February to 2 June 1958, Cunningham was at Alpha. In
April the station had to be moved one mile away to another floe because
the original one began to break up. It took 12 days to move the 22
buildings, to prepare another airstrip, and to get the scientific programs
underway again. From 4 April 1957, his first night on the ice, to 1
September 1958, Cunningham spent a total of about 250 days on the
polar ice cap.[25]

From the outset Cunningham had authority to exclude from the station any man, whether scientist or airman, unsuited for the station and
its objectives. By the end of August 1958, he had sent home two scientists
and two airmen.[26]

For his services to the Air Force during the International Geophysical
Year he was paid 30 dollars per day, "all of which," he wrote to the
Gaughans on 1 September 1958, "in a moment of sentimental generosity
I turn over to the new [Monroe] Catholic High School in Fairbanks.
The pastor told me recently I was the only one that keeps the school
above water, and they are hoping I will die soon so they can name
a room after me. But I have to admit I enjoy practically sinful good
health."

13 / Final Year: 1958-1959

At 11:15 a.m., 23 September 1958, Cunningham landed at Drift Station Alpha for what turned out to be his last stay there. He had come to Alpha to be with the men as the long polar night began to descend. Six weeks later in the gloom of early November, they made national headlines: "Ice Island Carrying 21 Breaks Apart," "Rescue Planes Set Out to Aid Group on Floe," "20 Men Airlifted from Polar Floe."[1]

On Sunday, 2 November, the floe on which Alpha was located — approximately 900 nautical miles northeast of Barrow and 250 nautical miles from the North Pole — was lashed by a polar storm so violent that it broke in two. The section with the runway, which alone made travel to and from the floe possible, broke away from the section on which the camp was pitched. It was evident that the camp would have to be abandoned without delay. That storm, following on the heels of one two weeks earlier, had reduced the Alpha floe to only 30 percent of its original size. It is reported that whenever the marooned men heard a noise like the roar of 100 freight trains they knew it meant a new crack in their floe. At each such boom Cunningham would pull on his parka and remark, "Well, let's get out and see how much real estate we have left."[2]

In a 16-foot fiberglass boat powered by a 40-horsepower outboard the 12 airmen and the eight scientists on Alpha crossed the two-mile-wide lead between the floes and repaired as best they could what was left of the runway for a hoped-for rescue plane to land on. For four days, however, owing to high winds, they were stranded on the camp floe — now a sheet of tortured ice roughly only 1000 feet square — awaiting rescue.

On Thursday, 6 November, two planes, a ski-equipped C-123 J-A twin-engine transport with two auxiliary jet engines and a C-54, took off from Harmon Air Force Base, Greenland, 600 nautical miles to the southeast of Drift Station Alpha. Notified by radio that rescuers would soon be there, the men at the station moved to the runway floe and

The cross near the North Pole indicates the location of the marooned men when Drift Station Alpha split in two on 2 November 1958. *(Oregon Province Archives)*

set out flares. By the eerie light of the flares flickering in the inky darkness of the polar night, the C-123 J-A landed without mishap. Seventeen minutes later, at 10:45 p.m., Anchorage time, despite the darkness, the high winds, and a temperature of minus 24 degrees, all were safely on board and ready for takeoff. Most of the scientific data collected up to that point were also on board. Cunningham, one of the first to land at Alpha, was the last to leave.[3]

From Alpha the men were flown first to Alert, an emergency field located on the northern coast of Ellesmere Island, for a refueling stop, then on to Thule, where they arrived at 8:00 a.m. on the seventh. While at Thule, Cunningham remarked, "all our prayers were answered by this plane" — terse words, yet words packed with relief and gratitude. Coming as they did from the man ultimately responsible for the safety of the men on Alpha, they were as sincere as they were simple. The rescued men left Thule the evening of the seventh, and arrived at Westover Air Force Base, Massachusetts, the following day. By early afternoon on the ninth, Cunningham was in New York City, where he spent five days.

In New York, Cunningham and the other rescued airmen were interviewed by Ed Sullivan for the Ed Sullivan TV show. Sullivan singled out Cunningham — wearing the uniform of an Air Force major — as "the man with the know-how."[4] The program was televised nationally on 16 November.

Cunningham also took time out to visit his cousin, Norine Mahoney,[5] and to be interviewed by the journalist Bob Considine. In his newspaper article, Considine described Cunningham as "a trim, bone-weary, nonchalant man of 52 who speaks with a clipped understatement that tends to leave one filled with both envy and unfulfillment."

From Considine's article we learn that Cunningham had charge of the movies and of running the projector on Alpha, and before that "big ice cube" was abandoned it was his duty to destroy — in the name of national security! — movies which had been airdropped to the men at Alpha. Cunningham is quoted as saying, "It was with great joy that I first burned an epic named *Be-bop Girl Goes Calypso*. There followed *Calypso Joe*. But I was sorry to see Judy Holliday's *Full of Life* go, and I mourned as I touched a match to *Gun Fight at the O K Corral*. A good movie."[6]

Cunningham revealed himself as a film critic also in several letters to the Gaughans. (In none of his letters do we come to know Cunningham the man better than in his letters to the Gaughans.) From a letter written to them on 4 September 1952, we learn that he went to see *The Greatest Show on Earth*. "But, it wasn't," he commented. "The acrobatics, which I love, were all cluttered up by jealousy and love, both of which are all right in the proper time, but out of place in the circus. There was a love scene with the principals sitting on bales of hay in the moonlight that was boring and pure waste of time. It must have lasted ten minutes and precluded some good juggling scenes."

Five years later, on 27 September 1957, he wrote to the Gaughans from Barrow, "If you have occasion to see a movie called *La Strada*, don't! We had it here last night, and it was so terrible I sat through it in sheer fascination. It's an Italian movie. The hero and heroine barely made the human race, and the plot was mixed up like a dog's breakfast."

What about Cunningham as poet? To the Gaughans, again from Barrow, he wrote on 28 July 1954, "Do you ever think about original sin? If you do, you must know that the snake was the prime cause. The garden of Eden was poorly located. Should have been in Alaska, where there are no snakes to tempt Eve to tempt Adam. Too cold for them."

After this preamble, he versified:

"In view of this, old Adam's fall, might never have occurred at all, If God had only chosen,
To situate that garden home at Anaktuvuk or at Nome —
Or some place else that's frozen.
Consider (how this makes me gasp!), if Eden had contained no asp, From death we'd be insured.
We'd have no tendency to sin, if only had that garden been
In Barrow, Tok, or Seward."

These were intended to be the last lines of the poem. The opening ones went as follows:

"In seven days, God made the world. He found it good, and, as it twirled, God manufactured Adam.
No kith did Adam have nor sib; so God excised from him a rib, and shaped up Adam's madam."

"I haven't figured out verses for in between yet," he concluded his letter to the Gaughans.

From 14 to 23 November 1958 Cunningham was on leave granted him by the Air Force, part of which he spent at Fort Ord, California, with what he called his "adopted stateside family," the Colonel J. Aaron Cook family. Having befriended the Cooks some years earlier at Fort Richardson, he gratefully accepted an invitation to rest in their home, and to meet for the first time, and pose with, four-year-old Thomas Patrick Cook, his namesake. The Gaughans, too, had named a son Thomas Patrick for Cunningham.

Cunningham returned to Alaska in late November, and from the 29th to 12 December he was at Ladd Air Force Base on what he described as "Ice Skate business."

Because of his appearance on the Ed Sullivan TV show and his name and picture appearing in newspapers all across the country, he was at this time truly a national figure, variously described as "hero of northern near-tragedy," "padre of the arctic ice," "indomitable Jesuit priest," "remarkable Jesuit," "Icy Jesuit," "arctic priest," and "expert on polar ice conditions." The widespread, favorable public exposure brought him a flood of mail from far and near. Friends and admirers wrote

Father Tom visiting his "adopted stateside family," Col. and Mrs. J. Aaron Cook and their four-year-old son, Thomas Patrick, his namesake, at Fort Ord, California, November 1958. *(Herald-AP photo. Oregon Province Archives)*

to him to tell him how thrilled they had been to see him on the Ed Sullivan program. Some teased him good-naturedly about being a national TV celebrity, and about having played hopscotch at the North Pole. "All America has heard of your recent escapades," wrote one. A fellow priest felt compelled to write him to compliment him on the fact that he had added to the glory of the Church by his "exemplary though adventurous and even charmed life."[7] A chaplain friend wrote him, "Knowing you, Tom, has been a real inspiration and a pleasure." From a high school stamp club president, who had read about him in the *American Weekly*, he received a request for autographed envelopes mailed at Barrow. A man wanted a polar bear skin. A lady in Virginia wrote him that she would be happy to send him anything that might contribute to his amusement or add a little to his comfort. From a Sister doing advanced degree work at St. Louis University came a request for information about the Eskimo diet. One woman wanted him to line up an "Eskimo pen friend" for her. An Army captain who had served with him in Nome asked him in a letter whether he would be interested in having the story of his life told in print and on the screen.

Hargreaves, the General Superior of the Alaska Mission, too, took note of Cunningham's achievements, and wrote to the Father General in Rome, John B. Janssens, "Fr. Thomas Cunningham received quite a bit of publicity in the secular press due to his work with the Air Force which had a scientific project in operation for over a year on the floating ice in the Arctic Ocean. Fr. Cunningham had much to say as to location of site, choice of men; and he did spiritual good by his words and example."[8]

From Washington, executive director of the National Academy of Sciences Hugh Odishaw wrote Cunningham: "The scientific personnel who recently returned from IGY Station Alpha following its breakup have repeatedly expressed their appreciation of the contributions which you made to the work at this station...I should like to express for the U.S. National Committee for the IGY and for myself personally our warm and sincere thanks for these tangible contributions to the US-IGY program at Station Alpha."[9]

The U.S. Air Force, too, knew again how to show itself grateful to Cunningham for his services during the final days of Alpha. On 10 March 1959 it awarded him the Air Force Commendation Medal for having "distinguished himself by meritorious service during the period 23 September 1958 to 7 November 1958 while serving as chaplain of Station Alpha...In spite of extremely adverse and hazardous living conditions, sub-zero temperatures, high winds, continuous darkness, and complete isolation, he provided religious and spiritual guidance, so essential to the well-being of personnel in such an environment, which contributed substantially to the continued compilation of valuable research data by scientists of the International Geophysical Year...By his spiritual direction, perseverance, and devotion to duty, Chaplain Cunningham has brought credit upon himself, the Alaskan Air Command, and the United States Air Force."

Cunningham wrote the following note at the bottom of a carbon copy of the above citation: "They pinned the medal on me in the presence of four generals and eleven colonels, and then took it back saying, 'It is the only one we have, and [we] might need it again.' "

"There is no question," wrote pilot William Gilmore to his friend "Rudy" on 29 April 1959, "about the fact that Father Tom was a great morale builder on Station A. The mere fact that he was there and knew so much about the Arctic was reassuring. He worked as hard and probably kept longer hours than most of the men. And, of course, he ministered to all the men irrespective of their faith.

USAF Brig. Gen. C.F. Necrason and Father Tom, wearing the Air Force Commendation Medal awarded him on 10 March 1959 for having "distinguished himself by meritorious service . . . while serving as chaplain of Station Alpha." *(U.S. Air Force photo. Oregon Province Archives)*

"He had a wonderful sense of humor to top it all off. You remember the first runway was really a fine one and 5000 feet long. I always made short field type landings though, since you could never be sure of the braking action. On one trip up Father Tom came up to the flight deck and gave me quite a lecture on how hard he had worked to build that runway and that he felt hurt by the fact that I apparently mistrusted his engineering ability because of the fact that I wasn't using but about half of it for landing. Halfway out beyond Barrow, Station A went off the air, and, as we supposed, it was because of a crack which knocked out their generators. It also knocked about 1500 feet off the runway. A strong cross wind and fresh snow made a slippery runway, and as it happened on that landing, although we touched down right on the end, we slid, weather cocked into the wind, the whole length of it and right up to the open water alongside the crack at the far end. Major [Joseph P.] Bilotta was screaming at me over the URC/4 to steer off onto the snow, and I sure was trying, but had no control. Anyway, we stopped. Then just sat and tried to get over the shakes before turning around to taxi back to the parking spot, when Father Tom stuck his head up front and paralyzed us all by saying, with a gleam in his eye, 'You don't have to always take an old priest seriously, you know!'"

No sooner was Drift Station Alpha abandoned, than the Air Force began to make plans for a new station. Predictably, it again wanted Cunningham's assistance, but in the late winter and early spring of 1959 drinking had once again become a problem in his life, and his Jesuit Superiors hesitated at first to let him take part in the reestablishment of a drift station. However, because it was thought he would have to help out for only about a month, and because the Air Force all but insisted on his services, Superiors allowed him to serve one more time as special advisor. By 14 April he was out on the ice again.[10]

By this time the Air Force had total confidence in his judgment regarding polar pack ice behavior. On 8 May 1959 USAF Brigadier General C.F. Necrason, Commander, Alaskan Air Command, sent out notice that Cunningham had been designated arctic advisor for the new "Ice Station Alpha II" and that he had the "specific responsibility for providing guidance on all matters concerning camp layout and construction, arctic survival, and arctic safety." Necrason wanted Cunningham to be heard as an authority, with power to command. So totally was Cunningham in charge of the safety of the station that he was able to write from it on 29 May to a nurse friend, Ellin Andress, "I can also close up the whole works, no questions asked, if I should think it necessary."

What inspired such confidence on the part of the Air Force in Cunningham's judgment in matters polar ice, according to Gilmore, was the fact that "Father Tom was able to make such accurate predictions of just where and when Station Alpha would crack. The original map he drew predicting cracks was almost a duplicate of one which was kept to show where the cracks actually were."

One thing that Cunningham insisted on when it came to setting up the new ice station was that power lines entering the buildings be of a quick disconnect type so that the lines would merely disconnect rather than break when ice movement occurred or when polar bears dragged their feet across them. It would be a simple matter to reconnect them when the ice was stable again. He had advocated such wiring for the old station, but his advice was not heeded. Actual events proved it to have been sound.[11]

One day, while Ice Station Alpha II was being set up, Cunningham was operating the one and only weasel in camp. On this self-propelled, tracked vehicle he was out making a map of the floe when he broke through a narrow lead of thin ice hidden under a thick layer of snow. "I lost everything, weasel and its contents," he wrote Ellin Andress, "and hated to tell the C.O. about it. I had to walk 2 miles home, and my clothes were frozen on me, so the C.O. took a tolerant attitude." The Air Force then sent two more weasels, one of the amphibious type, which Cunningham thought "very sarcastic of them." Crews of the C-124s teased him, "How's the water?" "Been swimming lately?" and the like. "The annoying part of the whole thing," wrote Cunningham, "is that I am the one who is not supposed to have accidents." There is no question that he liked the friendly teasing, and took it as a sign of the men's warm personal esteem for him.

He does not seem to have forgotten his Barrow parish when he was involved with the two ice stations. Gilmore, who piloted him frequently, wrote, "Several times, as we would be returning from the island and overflying Barrow because of weather, he would have us contact Wien-Barrow radio facilities and pass a message to insure that what fuel and food he had there — and wouldn't be using because we were overflying — would be distributed to the needy folk in the village."

As was his wont, Cunningham was generous with the "needy folk" of Barrow. Still, "some poor sinners," as he styled them, at times did not wait to be given food or fuel, but instead simply helped themselves, especially to his stove oil. At night — and it should be remembered, during the winter months Barrow had a great deal of night — they would "borrow some," by syphoning it out of his tank.[12] There were nights when he woke up shivering because his stove was cold, the fuel having run out unexpectedly, thanks to "some poor sinner's" borrowing again. When this happened, he would go across the road to the home of Mr. and Mrs. Edward F. Misiewicz, employees of the U.S. Weather Bureau, let himself in, and roll up in a blanket on the couch of their living room to sleep till morning.

One morning the lady of the house — not knowing that she had a guest on the couch — got up early to go to the kitchen. She was wearing her favorite, but old, well-worn, flannel nightgown. As she came through the living room, she suddenly noticed Cunningham eyeing her. There was a moment of silence, before he said, mock-seriously, "I didn't know you were so poor you couldn't afford a new nightgown. That one's definitely on its last legs. You'll never do much for anyone wearing *that.*"[13]

Notwithstanding their inopportune "borrowing" habits, Cunningham got along well with the Barrow Natives. He also had many friends among the whites of Barrow, and, as in Nome, he made a habit of "eating out" — of inviting himself to people's homes, to the Arctic Research Laboratory, to the Puget Sound and Drake camp, and to the hospital.

Although none of the Barrow hospital staff was Catholic, he went there every Friday for good fellowship and "a proper, Christian fish dinner." But he did not go empty-handed. In a zipper bag he took with him a pair of barber clippers, a comb, and shears to cut the hair of Dr. George S. Walter. Cunningham had a special admiration for this doctor because he was "working himself to death for the Natives."[14]

The 12th of August 1959 marked the 25th anniversary of Cunningham's ordination to the priesthood, but he made little of the occasion. To his cousin, Norine Mahoney, he wrote, in answer to her question what he wanted for his silver jubilee, "A Jesuit never thinks of a silver jubilee, let alone celebrates."[15] From Auckland, New Zealand, a grade school classmate wrote to him, "May I wish you great joy, happiness and every blessing on attaining the 25th year of your ordination to the priesthood. May God spare you for many more years to carry on the wonderful and heroic work you do amongst your people in the far distant North."[16] And James M. Liston, the archbishop of the Auckland diocese, took occasion to assure Cunningham of "prayers, felicitations and wishes."

Did Cunningham, after spending nearly a quarter of a century in priestly missionary work in northern Alaska, ever regret having volunteered for the Alaska Mission? It seems not. During his Barrow years he was in Anchorage once to speak at the monthly Day of Recollection for priests and Catholic chaplains from the various services. At the dinner held in the Fort Richardson Officers Club following the Recollection, he made the following remarks: "I am most grateful to you good priests and to your people who have done so much for me and my missionary work. But sometimes you seem to express sorrow for me because of certain apparent hardships in my work. You need never feel sorry for me because I am doing the work I chose and the work I love. As far as my Superiors are concerned, we have a mutual understanding that I may leave Alaska any time I so desire. But why would I want to leave such fine friends?"[17]

14 / Father Tom of the Arctic, R.I.P.: September 1959

"Fr. Cunningham, Arctic Priest, Dies," read a headline in the *San Francisco Chronicle* on 5 September 1959. Cunningham's name was again in the headlines of newspapers across the nation and on nationwide radio broadcasts, but this time to announce his death.

Cunningham had written from Barrow to his friends, the Gaughans, almost five years before, "I look forward to ending my days here, not immediately, you understand, but eventually. I will be 49 years old next month; not in the sere and yellow of life, it is true, but definitely on the downhill slide. I am hoping the Lord will give me another 25 years of Active Duty."[1] But the Lord decreed otherwise for Thomas Patrick Cunningham. The end came swiftly and without compromise. At Barrow, in his quonset hut dwelling, after morning Mass and breakfast, on 3 September 1959, without benefit of Last Rites, his colorful life's odyssey came to an abrupt end at the age of 53.

There were a few indications, however, immediately preceding his death that all was not well. On 23 August, newly arrived schoolteacher Frances Ross — daughter of Nome pioneer and boat captain Tom Ross, a close friend of Cunningham's from the day they first met in Nome in 1935 — had hurried over to St. Patrick's Mission in hopes of attending Sunday Mass. But when she got to the quonset church, she found a penciled note on the door to the effect that there would be no Mass that day. Nevertheless, she entered the church to pray. A small portable organ up front attracted her attention. Having once been an organist in Nome and on King Island, she decided to try it out. When she was halfway through the hymn *Tantum Ergo*, she noticed the door near the altar alcove open.

"A frail old man stood there, white whiskers on his cheeks and chin, a faded blue bathrobe thrown about his shoulders. He stared at me severely for a moment, then moved toward the center of the church, genuflected slowly. Banging the organ shut, I followed him out to the front entry.

" 'There won't be any Mass this morning,' he stated in a quiet, tired voice. 'I've been sick most of the night and wouldn't last through it.'

"Baffled as to his identity — 'this can't be Father Tom,' I thought blankly — we were shaking hands, and his face softened with a smile. 'Oh, Frances! I remember your father very well. Stop by tomorrow.'

"With the build-up my friends had given me, I was fully expecting to meet a powerful man of action, no less than six feet six inches tall, a vigorous and hearty athlete. I was not prepared to meet this thin, slightly stooped figure I faced now, who appeared to be more a hospital patient, scarcely ambulatory, than the polar hero he was."[2]

Then, on the following Sunday, 30 August, there was Mass, at 11:00 o'clock, which Frances Ross reported as follows:

"His customary whipcord suit and combat boots were replaced by a cassock in which, although ramrod straight, he appeared most thin and slight. As he lit the two altar candles, his steel-rimmed glasses seemed to increase his serious and withdrawn demeanor. Donning white vestments in the combination confessional-sacristy, he approached the altar to begin Mass.

"No man came forward from the congregation to serve. There must have been a dozen people in the congregation, non-Eskimo except for Flossie [Connery, one of Cunningham's Barrow converts] and another woman. No one gave the responses. It is to my regret that I did not answer Father Tom's '*Introibo*...'

"There was no music. Turning from the gospel side, Father announced, with a smile, that the *North Star* would arrive at Barrow that day at 12:45 p.m., the news for which all Barrow waited impatiently.

"A paperbound Steadman missal in his hand, Father read the epistle and gospel for the fifteenth Sunday after Pentecost. His thumb as a marker, he folded his fingers around the little book and began his sermon on St. Paul's message of charity.

"As well as I can remember, it went like this: 'We all have a cross to bear. Our job is to save our souls, not to beat our neighbors over the head about theirs. By our example we can do tremendous' (he pronounced it 'tremenjus') 'good. We don't know what grace God gives each soul; we don't know another's burdens nor the graces God gives to carry them. We must not meddle nor judge.'

"It occurred to me while he was preaching, 'This is Father Tom's apostolate, cutting through a person's beliefs to the soul itself.' Stripped of oratory, with insistence upon charity towards all, Father Tom spoke with direct simplicity. Deeply impressed, I sensed a degree of the basic affection that so many non-Catholics in particular felt toward him. Church affiliation did not stop Father Tom from establishing the warmest human ties. He reached out and won people on their own terms.

"In a new light I watched the priest proceed toward the Consecration. No collection was taken up. No bell rang. At communion we filed toward the alcove, kneeling there close to the altar. From the paten Father distributed the consecrated wafers. There was a profound intimacy; we were so few."[3]

On Wednesday, 2 September, Cunningham invited the Reverend Paul Bills of the Assembly of God Church to come over to St. Patrick's to get some potatoes and a lamb roast. When Bills went there the next day, Thursday, he received no response to his knock and left.[4] At 6:00 p.m., an Eskimo man from the Native store went to the rectory to deliver 36 drums of fuel oil. When he opened the door to ask where he should put it, he found Cunningham lying on the floor, and immediately ran to the hospital to report "a dead man in the cabin." Without delay Dr. Walter and two nurses went to investigate, found the stiffening body, bathed it, dressed it in sleeping clothes, and placed it in the unheated bedroom.

Around 9:15 that evening, Ross heard a breathless voice calling her. She opened the door of her living quarters to find an excited young woman. "I'm Liza, the nurse," she panted, trying to catch her breath, "and I've got bad news! It's Father Tom! He's dead — they found him at six o'clock tonight, coronary occlusion!"

Toward midnight Ross and the nurse Eliza Bridenbaugh, accompanied by a schoolteacher, went to the rectory. "His body was right here," said Eliza, as she pointed to a spot on the floor between the stove and cupboard, right at the door itself. "Dr. Walter," she added, "thinks he must have been getting ready to leave the house. He was dressed to go outdoors, and he was turning the oil low in the stove," for they found, nearby, a small screwdriver Cunningham had used to adjust the fuel intake. "Dr. Walter says he didn't suffer," Eliza added reassuringly. "It came fast — about 9:30 this morning."[5]

On Friday, 4 September, the commanding officer of the Air Force in Alaska, Lieutenant General Frank A. Armstrong, dispatched his personal plane to Barrow to pick up Father Tom's body for burial in Fairbanks. In the late afternoon, shrouded in driving snow, what was mortal of Cunningham — a slight mound under a blue Air Force blanket, lying on a stretcher, toes curled in black socks sticking out at one end, a wisp of grey hair at the other — was carried out of the quonset rectory he had built five years earlier to a truck waiting to drive his remains to the landing field for a last flight.[6] At the time of his death Cunningham held the rank of major in the Air Force Reserve. He had served the Air Force well and loved it, and it was a fitting gesture on its part that it should give him his last ride, bring him to his final resting place.

As the news of his death reached the public, telegrams and letters of condolences began to pour into Fairbanks — to Bishop Gleeson and Cunningham's fellow Jesuits. From the austerity of Barrow in the Arctic to the splendor of the nation's capitol in Washington, Father Tom was mourned, and his death noted and discussed by many people — obscure and prominent — and by local and national periodicals. Cunningham's legions of friends and acquaintances deluged Boileau with letters. Boileau, who took charge of Cunningham's affairs, also solicited materials and information about him, since he intended to write his biography. The tributes to Cunningham, and sentiments expressed were universal: he was much loved and would be sorely missed.[7]

The body of the man who throughout his life overtaxed his strength in helping others, who literally burned himself out in the service of God and fellow man, lying now in a simple grey casket — unadorned except for a small crucifix which well symbolized his life and work — was moved into Immaculate Conception Church at 4:00 p.m. on Monday, 7 September, to lie in state. That evening many lay people, priests, and nuns gathered there to pray the rosary and to recite the Office for the Dead. The body, dressed in priestly vestments and bathed in the mellow light of six flickering candles, was left in the church overnight.

On Tuesday morning, at 10:00 o'clock, a Solemn Pontifical Requiem Mass was celebrated by Bishop Gleeson. The church was crowded with people from all walks of life, who came to pay their last respects to the much admired priest, Air Force officer, fellow man. Priests, chaplains, and nuns from St. Joseph's Hospital and the parochial schools filled the sanctuary and front pews. Air Force personnel, including Brigadier General Gordon H. Austin, Commander, 11th Air Division, civic leaders, and laity filled the church to overflowing. Nurses flew from Elmendorf, and came from Ladd.

The eulogy was delivered by Boileau, who traced the adventurous life of the Arctic priest from its rural beginnings in New Zealand to

The U.S. Air Force salutes the remains of Chaplain Cunningham as they are being carried out of Immaculate Conception Church, Fairbanks, on their way to their last resting place, 8 September 1959. *(Photo by Jim Young for Phil's Photos. Oregon Province Archives)*

Australia, Ireland, Belgium, Spokane, Holy Cross, Montreal, Nome, Little Diomede; then to service in the Army and Air Force; to Kotzebue and, finally, to Barrow. A chorus of military chaplains sang the responses. At the end of the hour-long Mass, two airmen came forward, closed the casket, and draped a 49-star flag over it. (One wonders, did that new 49th star weigh heavily on Cunningham? He had opposed statehood and voted against it.[8]) To the tolling of bells the casket was then carried out to be taken to the cemetery. The day was mild and sunny, with scattered clouds. The birches next to the church and those next to the Jesuit plot in the cemetery off Clay Street were in the first gold of autumn.

Many who attended the funeral Mass were also present at the graveside ceremonies, which were also conducted by Bishop Gleeson. The same chorus that had sung the responses in the church chanted the Latin *Benedictus.* Taps sounded. A military guard of honor from Ladd Air Force Base fired off a three-round rifle salute. A nurse shed a last tear. Airmen folded the flag and presented it to Bishop Gleeson. Slowly people began to file out of the cemetery. Priests and nuns in black and white were the last to leave.

In the land of his birth, too, in faraway New Zealand, a Solemn Requiem Mass was celebrated commemorating Father Tom's death. On 10 September the bishop of the Diocese of Dunedin, 40 priests, and the students of Holy Cross College which Cunningham had attended, gathered in his home town of Mosgiel to pay tribute to their fellow priest, former classmate, and countryman. Also present were his three brothers and their families, but his 90-year-old stepmother was too feeble to attend.[9]

At the time of his death, Cunningham was still remembered, and looked upon as a folk hero among the Catholics of New Zealand. The editor of the *N. Z. Tablet* wrote that "Father Tom is regarded in this country as one of the greatest of New Zealand's sons and a specially heroic missionary."[10]

Although Barrow had been Cunningham's home for only five years, his death "hit Barrow hard." The area around St. Patrick's "seemed abandoned, quarantined." White Catholic parishioners mourned him especially, but Barrow Eskimos and non-Catholics also grieved at his death. There were Eskimos like Alice Allan Kill Bear who said that, though they were not Catholic, he gave them food when they needed it, and helped send her daughter to school in Portland, Oregon; and Protestant ministers, like the Reverend Bills, who said that Father Cunningham was "a fine man [who] used to say, 'We're all working in the Lord's Vineyard.' "[11]

Cunningham made few Eskimo converts in Barrow; nevertheless, he left his mark — and his name — on that community. St. Patrick's Church and rectory front on Cunningham Street, one of the few Barrow streets to bear a non-Eskimo name. The Catholic community of Barrow has outgrown the church he built, and there is talk about building a new and larger one.

On Little Diomede Island, where Cunningham put in some of his best years as a missionary, and which he called his "first love," a new church was built in 1978 to accommodate a growing congregation. Eskimo men and women of Diomede whom he instructed in the Catholic faith have become active participants in a diocesan-wide renewal process initiated by the Diocese of Fairbanks.

Of all the words written about Cunningham at his death, probably none would have pleased him more than those in the 1960 Monroe Catholic High School annual, the *Aurigena*, which the students dedicated to the memory of "the great missionary and educator, Father Cunningham, whose three great loves were the Missions, the Military, and Monroe." Much of the money he had earned as an ice expert he contributed to this new school, which has continued to flourish as a private school with high academic standards.

Soon after his death, a "Father Tom Cunningham Scholarship" was established at Monroe. Air Force nurses, whom he had befriended at the 5005th hospital at Elmendorf during the years 1951-1952, took much of the initiative in establishing this scholarship, and were the first to make generous contributions to it. There are numerous letters in the Cunningham file, written both by him and by nurses, that attest to the warm love that existed between them. "Father Tom," wrote one nurse, "was not only the nurses' favorite, but also the nurses' pet. When Father Tom was admitted to the hospital with pneumonia, the nurses tried to outsmart each other to see who could do the most for Father Tom. I can remember very clearly how he would blush when the nurses brought him clean pajamas. He tried to act embarrassed, but deep down he really loved all the attention that he was getting."[12]

For all the dramatic adventures of his adult life and the national recognition he received toward the end of it, Cunningham always remained basically a simple man, just "Father Tom." It was this simplicity and goodness of heart, grounded in a deep, personal spirituality, that drew people of all walks of life to him and made him so effective as a man and a priest, and so universally loved.

Cunningham, who never rested while alive, found his final resting place just a few feet from that of Father Bellarmine Lafortune who, a quarter of a century earlier, had introduced him to missionary work among the Eskimos. What Cunningham wrote in the King Island diary about Lafortune at the time of the latter's death can fittingly be written about Cunningham himself, "He was a good man to have in this world."

Notes

Chapter 1

1. Letter, Cunningham to Margaret Mahoney, Dublin, 15 September 1927. Almost all the original, unpublished materials referred to in these notes — other than the letters to Renner and the transcripts of interviews conducted by him — are deposited in the Oregon Province Archives of the Society of Jesus, housed in the Crosby Library of Gonzaga University, Spokane, Washington, and in the Jesuit Provincial Archives in Portland, Oregon.
2. Letters, Theresa Kenny to George T. Boileau, S.J., Auckland, N.Z., 11 April 1962; John E. Cunningham to Boileau, Dunedin, N.Z., [1960].
3. Letters, Kenny to Boileau, Auckland, N.Z., 11 April 1962; Rev. T.J. Liddy to Renner, Mosgiel, N.Z., 1 February 1983.
4. Letter, Thomas J. Martin, S.J., to Renner, Dublin, 9 October 1972.
5. "Notes on Fr. Thomas Cunningham, S.J., dictated by Fr. Joseph Hurley, S.J.," Dublin, n.d., in letter, Matthew Meade, S.J., to Renner, Dublin, 17 June 1981; letter, Henry P. O'Brien, S.J., to Renner, Phoenix, 19 October 1972.
6. Letter, Cunningham to "Mum & Dad," Eegenhoven, 24 September 1927.
7. Letter, Cunningham to "Mum & Dad," Eegenhoven, 9 October 1927.
8. Letter, Cunningham to "Mum & Dad," Eegenhoven, 30 October 1927.
9. See 7 above.
10. See 8 above.
11. Ibid.
12. Letter, Cunningham to "Mum & Dad," Eegenhoven, 20 November 1927.
13. Ibid.
14. Ibid.
15. Ibid.

16. Letters, Cunningham to "Mum & Dad," Eegenhoven, 11 March 1929; Cunningham to "Mum & Dad," Hillyard, WA., 19 December 1929.
17. Letter, Cunningham to "Mum & Dad," Eegenhoven, 19 March 1929.
18. Letter, Cunningham to "Mum & Dad," Eegenhoven, 19 March 1928.
19. Ibid.
20. Letter, Cunningham to "Mum & Dad," Eegenhoven, 14 April 1929.
21. "Notes on Fr. Thomas Cunningham, S.J., dictated by Fr. Joseph Hurley, S.J."
22. Letter, Cunningham to "Mum & Dad," Eegenhoven, 19 March 1928.
23. Letter, Cunningham to "Mum & Dad," Eegenhoven, 14 April 1929.
24. Letter, Cunningham to "Mum & Dad," Eegenhoven, 20 May 1929.
25. From tape deposited in the Oregon Province Archives.
26. See 19 December 1929 letter in 16 above.
27. *Oregon Jesuit*, Vol. 27, 1958, p.7.
28. Letters, Harold O. Small, S.J., to Renner, Seattle, 23 August 1982; Cunningham to "Mum & Dad," Hillyard, WA., 19 December 1929.
29. Letters, Cunningham to "Mum & Dad," Hillyard, 16 February 1930; Cunningham to "Mum & Dad," Hillyard, 7 April 1930.
30. See letter, 16 February 1930, in 29 above.
31. Ibid; see letter, 19 December 1929, in 16 above.
32. See letter, 19 December 1929, in 16 above; interview with Joseph P. Logan, S.J., Portland, OR., 10 March 1981.
33. See letter, 7 April 1930, in 29 above.

Chapter 2

1. Letter, Cunningham to *St. Joseph's Sheaf*, Holy Cross, 3 November 1930, published in *St. Joseph's Sheaf*, June 1931, p. 300.
2. See Calasanctius 1947, *passim;* Renner 1979a; Renner 1980-81; interview with George J. Feltes, S.J., Fairbanks, 18 October 1982.
3. See 1 above.
4. Interview with Logan, Portland, 10 March 1981.
5. Letters, Cunningham to John and Gerry Gaughan, Barrow, 27 September 1957; Norine Mahoney to Boileau, New York, 25 February 1960.
6. Interview with Erwin J. Toner, S.J., Spokane, 5 March 1981.
7. Letter, Robert Picard, S.J., to Renner, Montreal, 5 April 1981.

Chapter 3

1. For the history of the Catholic Church in Nome, see Renner 1979b, *passim.*

2. "Nome Diary," p. 166.
3. Ibid., p. 167.
4. Letters, Cunningham to Joseph R. Crimont, S.J., Nome, 26 February 1936; Cunningham to *Jesuit Missions*, Nome, 3 March 1936, published in *Jesuit Missions*, Vol. 10, 1936, p. 161.
5. "Nome Diary," pp. 167, 168; "Holy Cross Diary," p. 466.
6. For a general history of the Pilgrim Springs Mission, see Renner 1977-78; Renner 1979b, pp. 40-53, 160-61; letter, Edward J. Cunningham, S.J., to Crimont, Pilgrim Springs, 3 May 1936.
7. "Nome Diary," p. 168.
8. Letter, Ann L. Walsh to Renner, Fairbanks, 2 March 1981.
9. Letter, James M. Walsh to Renner, Seattle, 27 August 1981; Anable 1981.
10. "Nome Diary," p. 168.
11. Quoted in letter, Meade to Renner, Dublin, 17 June 1981.
12. Letters, Bellarmine Lafortune, S.J., to Crimont, Nome, 18 August 1936; James Walsh to Renner, Seattle, 27 August 1981.
13. Letters, Walter J. Fitzgerald, S.J., to Crimont, Portland, 27 March 1936; 26 February 1936 in 4 above; 18 August 1936 in 12 above; "Nome Diary," p. 169.

Chapter 4

1. Bogojavlensky 1969, p. 8.
2. See Jenness 1929; Renner 1975-76.
3. Bogojavlensky 1969, p. 42; see Renner 1979b, pp. 14-15, 94-97.
4. "Little Diomede Diary," p. 1.
5. Anable 1981; Ross 1959, p. 13.
6. Letter, Segundo Llorente, S.J., to Renner, Moses Lake, WA., 20 December 1980.
7. Letters, Cunningham to John Cunningham, Diomede, [1938]; Cunningham to Paul C. O'Connor, S.J., Diomede, 28 March 1938.
8. Letters, Cunningham to Adélard Dugré, S.J., Diomede, 29 March 1938; Thomas F. Carlin, S.J., to Renner, Diomede, 16 July 1981.
9. "Little Diomede Diary," p. 9.
10. Ibid., pp. 10, 21.
11. See 29 March 1938 letter in 8 above.
12. Cunningham 1959.
13. Letter, Cunningham to *Jesuit Missions*, Nome, 23 September 1937, published in *Jesuit Missions*, Vol. 11, 1937, pp. 301-02.

14. "Nome Diary," p. 171.
15. Letter, Ann Walsh to Renner, Fairbanks, 2 March 1981; interview with James Walsh, Fairbanks, 14 July 1982.
16. See 6 above.
17. Letter, Mary Kelly to Renner, Medford, OR., 17 December 1982.
18. "Nome Diary," p. 173.

Chapter 5

1. "Little Diomede Diary," p. 11.
2. Ménager 1937, p. 201.
3. Letter, Cunningham to *Jesuit Missions*, Diomede, n.d., published in *Jesuit Missions*, Vol. 12, 1938, p. 191.
4. Letters, Joseph F. McElmeel, S.J., to Crimont, Nome, 10 July 1938; McElmeel to Crimont, Pilgrim Springs, 22 July 1938.
5. See 3 above.
6. Letter, Cunningham to Dugré, Diomede, 29 March 1938.
7. Letter, Cunningham to John Cunningham, Diomede, [1938].
8. See also letter, Cunningham to William G. Levasseur, S.J., Diomede, 13 April 1939; letter, Cunningham to O'Connor, Nome, 3 August 1938.
9. See Eide 1952, *passim;* Hawkes 1913, *passim;* Renner 1979b, *passim.*
10. Letter, Lafortune to Levasseur, Nome, 4 July 1938.
11. "Nome Diary," p. 186.
12. Letter, Llorente to Renner, Moses Lake, 20 December 1980.

Chapter 6

1. Letter, Cunningham to "Fr. John," Diomede, 20 October 1938.
2. See Alexander 1939; interview with Anable, Fairbanks, 12 November 1982.
3. On 2 March 1949 Cunningham wrote from King Island to Renner, "I remember back in 1938 I learned in June of the new pope, provincial and bishop. All three had been in office some time."
4. Letter, Llorente to Renner, Moses Lake, 20 December 1980.
5. Letter, Cunningham to William G. Elliott, S.J., St. Regis Mission, Quebec, 13 March 1940.
6. See letters, Norman E. Donohue, S.J., to Small, Bethel, 17 October 1953; Bernard F. McMeel, S.J., to Henry G. Hargreaves, S.J., Barrow, 1 April 1959.
7. Letter, McElmeel to Fitzgerald, Nome, 7 March 1940.

8. Letter, Crimont to Elliott, Juneau, 2 May 1940.

Chapter 7

1. Letters, Cunningham to Elliott, Nome, 27 July 1940; McElmeel to Fitzgerald, Nulato, 15 September 1940; J. Phillips, S.J., to Editor, *The New Zealand Tablet*, [1940].
2. Letter, Edward Cunningham to "Dear Bishop," Pilgrim Springs, 14 November 1940.
3. Letter, Fitzgerald to Crimont, Nome, 24 July 1941.
4. Letter, Cunningham to the Gaughans, "On Ptarmigan Flight," 1 September 1958.
5. "The Last Pagan," news item in *Jesuit Missions*, Vol. 16, 1942, p. 132.
6. Letter, Cunningham to John Cunningham, Diomede, [1938].
7. Interview with Edmund A. Anable, S.J., Fairbanks, 21 November 1982.
8. Letter, Edward J. Fortier to Renner, Anchorage, 2 October 1982.
9. Letters, Cunningham to Francis J. Curran, S.J., Nome, 12 March 1942; Cunningham to Crimont, Nome, 13 March 1942.
10. Letter, Fitzgerald to Crimont, Nome, 26 July 1941.
11. See Renner 1979b, pp. 160-61.
12. Letter, Cunningham to Crimont, Pilgrim Springs, 12 June 1942. See also O'Connor 1943.
13. O'Connor 1943; Potter 1977, p. 180.
14. Letter, Fitzgerald to Crimont, Anchorage, 21 January 1943.
15. Anable 1981; interview with Anable, Fairbanks, 26 November 1982; "The Army is Grateful," news item in *Jesuit Missions*, Vol. 17, 1943, p. 208.
16. Ibid.; letter, Fitzgerald to Edwin W. Jones, Fairbanks, 3 June 1943.
17. Letter, Claude M. Hirst to Crimont, Juneau, 16 August 1943.
18. Letters, Crimont to Fitzgerald, Juneau, 23 February 1944; Fitzgerald to McElmeel, Fairbanks, 26 February 1944; Fitzgerald to Leopold J. Robinson, S.J., Fairbanks, 28 February 1944; Fitzgerald to McElmeel, Fairbanks, 20 March 1944.
19. Letter, Cunningham to Fitzgerald, Nome, 8 May 1944.
20. Interview with Anable, Fairbanks, 7 November 1982.
21. Letters, Anable to Crimont, Nome, 20 April 1944; Cunningham to Fitzgerald, Nome, 27 April and 8 May 1944; Cunningham to Crimont, Nome, 29 August 1944; Fitzgerald to Crimont, Akulurak, 12 December 1944.

Chapter 8

1. Letter, Cunningham to Elliott, Diomede, 26 January 1942.
2. Letter, Fitzgerald to Jones, Fairbanks, 3 June 1943.
3. Letter, Crimont to Fitzgerald, Juneau, 20 February 1944.
4. Letter, Crimont to Fitzgerald, Juneau, 23 February 1944.
5. Letter, Bernard R. Hubbard, S.J., to Crimont, Nome, 3 September 1944.
6. Letters, Fitzgerald to Crimont, Fairbanks, 16 March 1944; Fitzgerald to Crimont, Akulurak, 12 December 1944.
7. See also letter, Fitzgerald to John F. Dougherty, S.J., Ketchikan, 11 May 1945.
8. Anable 1981; "List of Papers," serial number 17, in the Cunningham archive file; letter, Rev. Patrick J. Ryan to Fitzgerald, Washington, 6 May 1946.
9. Interview with Anable, Fairbanks, 15 January 1983.
10. Interview with Anable, Fairbanks, 17 December 1982.
11. Roseberry 1959, p. 2.
12. Letters, Cunningham to Fitzgerald, Minneapolis, received 4 May 1945; Cunningham to Fitzgerald, Atsugi AFB, 21 August 1946.
13. Letters, Ryan to Fitzgerald, Washington, 6 May 1946; Fitzgerald to Robinson, Fairbanks, 15 March 1944.
14. Letter, Cunningham to Small, King Island, 4 March 1949.
15. Interview with James Walsh, Fairbanks, 14 July 1982.
16. See letter, 21 August 1946, 12 above.
17. Letters, Fitzgerald to Anable, Juneau, 17 April 1946; Fitzgerald to Adjutant General, War Department, Juneau, 3 June 1946; Ryan to Fitzgerald, Washington, 6 May 1945.
18. Letter, J. Willard Wagner to Cunningham, Fort Lewis, WA., 9 September 1946.
19. Letter, Cunningham to Fitzgerald, Nome, 3 October 1946.

Chapter 9

1. Letter, Cunningham to Fitzgerald, Nome, 3 October 1946.
2. Letter, Cunningham to Crimont, Nome, 29 August 1944.
3. "Saint Patrick, Eskimo Patron," news item in *Jesuit Missions*, Vol. 17, 1943, p. 68.
4. See Renner 1979b, p. 147; letter, Cunningham to Joseph Waddel, S.J., King Island, 30 April 1948; "Nome Diary," p. 7.

5. See Renner 1979b, pp. 158-59.
6. Letter, Cunningham to Small, King Island, 29 April 1948.
7. Letter, Cunningham to *Irish Province News*, King Island, 5 March 1948, published in *Irish Province News*, Vol. 5, 1948, pp. 319-21.
8. Ross 1959, p. 2.
9. "King Island Diary," p. 39; letter, Cunningham to Renner, King Island, 17 March 1948.
10. Letter, Cunningham to Dugré, Diomede, 29 March 1938; *"Eskimo Dictionary,"* news item in *Jesuit Missions*, Vol. 13, 1939, p. 218.
11. Ross 1959, pp. 12-13.
12. Letter, Gerry Gaughan to Renner, Shawnee Mission, KS., 13 January 1983.
13. Letter, Lawrence D. Kaplan to Renner, Fairbanks, 9 December 1982.
14. See Ray 1961 and 1977, both *passim*.
15. Letter, Cunningham to Renner, King Island, 2 March 1949.
16. Fortier 1978, pp. 32-33.
17. Ibid.
18. "King Island Diary," p. 76.
19. Letter, Cunningham to Small, King Island, 4 March 1949.
20. Letter, Jack E. Gibson to Cunningham, Newport, R.I., 17 December 1956.
21. Letter, Gibson to Boileau, Long Beach, CA., 19 February 1960.
22. "King Island Diary," pp. 78-79.
23. Letters, Cunningham to Small, King Island, 13 October 1949; John W. Arnette to Cunningham, Elmendorf AFB, 5 October 1949; "King Island Diary," p. 83.
24. Hall 1945, p. 205.
25. Letters, Cunningham to *Jesuit Missions*, Diomede, n.d., published in *Jesuit Missions*, Vol. 12, 1938, p. 191; Cunningham to Buchanan, Diomede, 14 November 1938.
26. "King Island Diary," p. 97; letters, Cunningham to "Adjutant General," Washington, D.C., Fort Richardson, 29 September 1949; Edward F. Witsell to Cunningham, Washington, 27 January 1950.
27. "King Island Diary," pp. 108-09.

Chapter 10

1. Cunningham 1951.
2. Letter, Cunningham to the Gaughans, "Polar Ice Pack," 27 February 1951.
3. See 1 above.
4. Letter, Cunningham to the Gaughans, Fairbanks, 4 September 1952.
5. Cunningham 1959; letters, Elliott to Renner, Cave Junction, OR., 1 August 1982; Cunningham to Elliott, Diomede, 26 January 1942.
6. Letter, Llorente to Renner, Moses Lake, 20 December 1980.
7. Letter, Ethel Vogen to Boileau, Minneapolis, 16 April 1961.
8. Donohue 1953, p. 7.
9. See Renner 1979b, pp. 45-48.
10. Letter, John M. Geary to Cunningham, Ladd AFB, 3 May 1951; "Nome Diary," p. 21; interview with George E. Carroll, S.J., Fairbanks, 16 November 1982.
11. Miller 1953, p. 10.
12. Ibid., pp. 7-8.
13. News item in *Woodstock Letters*, Vol. 75, 1946, p. 175.
14. Interview with Anable, Fairbanks, 17 November 1982; letter, Gerry Gaughan to Renner, Shawnee Mission, 13 January 1983.
15. Letter, Cunningham to Renner, King Island, 2 March 1949.
16. Letter, Gerry Gaughan to Renner, Shawnee Mission, 13 January 1983.
17. Ross 1959, p. 2.
18. See 4 above.
19. Ibid.

Chapter 11

1. Letter, Cunningham to the Gaughans, Fairbanks, 4 September 1952.
2. "Fairbanks Diary," p. 74; "King Island Diary," p. 117.
3. See 1 above.
4. "Nome Diary," p. 25; letter, Cunningham to the Gaughans, Barrow, 16 April 1953; "Little Diomede Diary," p. 23.
5. Letter, Cunningham to the Gaughans, Barrow, 16 April 1953.
6. Letter, Donohue to Small, Bethel, 17 October 1953.
7. "Little Diomede Diary," p. 27.

Chapter 12

1. Letter, Francis A. Barnum, S.J., to *Woodstock Letters*, Washington, n.d., published in *Woodstock Letters*, Vol. 27, 1898, pp. 354-56.
2. See wallet-size laminated plastic card, dated 23 November 1954, in the Cunningham archive file; letter, Rev. Paul J. Giegerich to Boileau, Tucson, 13 February 1960.
3. Letter, Cunningham to the Gaughans, Barrow, 16 April 1953.
4. "Barrow Diary," p. 3; letter, McMeel to Renner, Hays, MT., 18 March 1981.
5. Letter, Cunningham to James U. Conwell, S.J., Barrow, 16 August 1954; Ross 1959, pp. 18-19; "Barrow Diary," p. 5.
6. Letter, Helen Carroll to Boileau, Alexandria, VA., 15 February 1960.
7. Letter, Cunningham to the Gaughans, Barrow, 12 October 1956.
8. Cunningham 1959.
9. Letter, Cunningham to the Gaughans, Barrow, 26 January 1955.
10. See Barrow Baptismal Record.
11. "Barrow Diary," p. 7.
12. See Fletcher 1953; Calvert 1960, p. 110.
13. Letter, Cunningham to Boileau, 80° 30' N., 148° W., 6 April 1957.
14. Letter, Cunningham to Mark A. Gaffney, S.J., 80° 30' N., 158° 40' W., 18 May 1957.
15. Letter, Cunningham to John Cunningham, "Ice Skate," 27 May 1957; Weeks 1965, p. 68.
16. Letter, Cunningham to John Cunningham, "Ice Skate," 27 May 1957.
17. News item, *The Alaska Sportsman*, Vol. 25, 1959, p. 23.
18. See 16 above.
19. Weeks 1965, p. 70; *Fairbanks Daily News-Miner*, 23 May 1957; letter, Cunningham to Toner, 80° 40' N., 160° 17' W., 27 May 1957.
20. "The Ice Man is a Priest," editorial in *Jesuit Missions*, Vol. 31, 1957, pp. 1-2.
21. See 14 above.
22. Letter, Cunningham to Conwell, Barrow, 10 August 1957; *DEWline Polar Echos*, Vol. 2, 1957, pp. 5, 9.
23. See 16 above.
24. Letter, Cunningham to Ellin Andress, "Ice Skate," 29 May 1959.
25. Letters, Cunningham to Norine Mahoney, Barrow, 6 July 1958; Cunningham to the Gaughans, "On Ptarmigan Flight," 1 September 1958.
26. Letter to Gaughans, in 25 above.

Chapter 13

1. See Cunningham's 16 September to 12 December 1958 handwritten notes in his archive file; *The Spokesman-Review*, 6 and 7 November 1958; *Spokane Daily Chronicle*, 7 November 1958.
2. Roseberry 1959, p. 2.
3. *The Alaska Sportsman*, Vol. 25, 1959, p. 23; letter, Cunningham to Andress, "Ice Skate," 29 May 1959; *Spokane Daily Chronicle*, 7 November 1958.
4. Ross 1959, p. 1.
5. Letter, Norine Mahoney to Boileau, New York, 25 February 1960.
6. *New York Journal-American*, 17 November 1958.
7. Letter, Giegerich to Cunningham, Tucson, [1958].
8. Letter, Hargreaves to John B. Janssens, S.J., Bethel, 17 February 1959.
9. Letter, Hugh Odishaw to Cunningham, Washington, 2 December 1958.
10. Letters, Hargreaves to Boileau, Bethel, 23 March 1959; McMeel to Hargreaves, Barrow, 1 April 1959; Hargreaves to Janssens, St. Marys, 26 May 1959; Cunningham to Andress, "Ice Skate," 29 May 1959.
11. Letter, William Gilmore to "Rudy," San Leandro, CA., 29 April 1959.
12. Ross 1959, p. 29.
13. Letter, Edith Misiewicz Curry to Renner, Fairbanks, 9 April 1979.
14. Ross 1959, p. 18.
15. See 5 above.
16. Letter, Theresa Kenny to Cunningham, Auckland, 10 August 1959.
17. Letter, Giegerich to Boileau, Tucson, 13 February 1960.

Chapter 14

1. Letter, Cunningham to the Gaughans, Barrow, 26 January 1955.
2. Ross 1959, p. 5.
3. Ibid., pp. 19-20.
4. Bills 1980, p. 108.
5. Ross 1959, pp. 23-25.
6. Ibid., p. 26.
7. Over and over the same sentiments were expressed: "I was crushed when I heard of Father Tom's death...left us in a state of shock...am just most distressed to pick up the morning's paper and read of Fr. Tom's death...felt such a deep personal loss at his going...most

saddened...very sad to learn that that great man had left this earth...God called him home. His work was done."

His friends in Alaska had similar thoughts: "Alaska will not be the same without him...the best friend I ever had...one of those rare men who do everything well, and in the very doing win all hearts...a saint if ever there was one...a rugged, kindly, lovable Jesuit...one of the greatest persons I have ever known...an inspiration...a great and most humble man...a most fine, gentle person...a genial unselfish friend and a courageous and resourceful man of action...liked and loved by all who came in contact with him...a member of the family...slight in stature, soft-spoken, but there was a strength of character that went out from the man...a finished *raconteur*...such a sparkling personality...a wonderful priest."

Lowell Thomas, who had given Cunningham a small Bulova watch set in a miniature Firestone rubber tire (Ross 1959, p. 14), telegraphed Lewis N. Doyle, S.J., principal of Monroe Catholic High School: "Have just heard from Generals Armstrong and Necrason about the death of Father Cunningham. Am sure this is because he gave himself so unsparingly. He was one of the most impressive men I ever knew. I wish such a wonderful man could have lived to be as old as Methuselah."

Armstrong telegraphed Doyle: "Father Tom was beloved by all who knew him and one of my dearest friends. His death has stunned all who knew him, and we will mourn his passing with deep regret. His unselfish contributions to the country he loved so well took their toll. Upon behalf of my command, I extend sympathies."

On 5 September the honorable Ernest Gruening, Senator from Alaska, paid tribute to him in the U. S. Senate. His remarks printed in the *Congressional Record:* "Mr. President, a noble and gallant figure has passed from the Alaska scene. He is the Reverend Thomas Cunningham, S.J., known far and wide throughout Arctic Alaska as 'Father Tom'...Now this devoted servant of God and of his fellow men has gone to his reward, but the memory of his courage — physical and moral — and his great friendliness, will linger to the end of the days of all who knew him" (*Congressional Record Appendix*, A7785).

His obituary appeared in the *New York Times* on 5 September 1959, and *Time* and *Newsweek* magazines also noted his death.

8. Cunningham 1959.

9. Letters, John Cunningham to Toner, Dunedin, N.Z., 8 October 1959; John Cunningham to Boileau, Dunedin, 5 January 1960; Kenny to Boileau, Auckland, 11 April 1962.

10. Letter, Rev. Francis D. O'Dea to Father Chapman, Dunedin, 18 September 1959.

11. Ross 1959, pp. 27-28; Bills 1980, p. 108.

12. Letter, Nancy Leftenant to Boileau, Wiesbaden, Germany, 16 February 1960.

Sources Consulted

Alexander, Calvert, S.J.
1939 "Mystery Man." *Jesuit Missions* 13(no.9):237.
Anable, Edmund A., S.J.
1981 "Rev. Thomas Cunningham, S.J." Typed manuscript in Renner's possession.
Bailey, Alfred M.
1971 *Field Work of a Museum Naturalist, 1919-1922.*
Denver Museum of Natural History, Denver, Colorado.
"Barrow Diary"
1954-59
Bills, Paul
1980 *Alaska.* Springfield, MO.: Gospel Publishing House.
Bogojavlensky, Sergei
1969 "Imaangmiut Eskimo Careers: Skinboats in Bering Strait."
Ph.D. dissertation, Harvard University.
Burg, Amos
1952 "North Star Cruises Alaska's Wild West." *National Geographic Magazine* 102(no.1):57-86.
Calasanctius, Sister Mary Joseph
1947 *The Voice of Alaska.* Lachine, Quebec: Saint Ann's Press.
Calvert, James
1960 *Surface at the Pole.* New York: McGraw Hill Co.
Carlson, Gerald F.
1966 *Two on the Rocks.* New York: McKay.
Cunningham, Thomas P., S.J.
1951 "Report on Ice Conditions During Polar Ice Cap Project."
Typed manuscript.
1959 "Address to the Women's Sodality of Elmendorf Air Force Base."
Tape recording, not transcribed.
Donohue, Norman E., S.J.
1953 "Visitation of the Mission of Northern Alaska. Feb. 2 to March 10, 1953." Typed manuscript.

Eide, Arthur H.
1952 *Drums of Diomede.* Hollywood: House-Warven.
"Fairbanks Diary"
1930-60
Fletcher, Joseph O.
1953 "Three Months on an Arctic Ice Island." *National Geographic Magazine* 103(no.4):489-504.
Fortier, Edward J.
1978 *One Survived.* Anchorage: Alaska Northwest Publishing Co.
Hall, George L.
1945 *Sometime Again.* Seattle: Superior Publishing Co.
Hawkes, Ernest W.
1913 "The Cliff-Dwellers of the Arctic." *Wide World Magazine,* Vol. 30, February, pp. 377-382; March, pp. 454-461; April, pp. 582-588.
"Holy Cross Diary"
1930-60
Hopkins, David M., ed.
1967 *The Bering Land Bridge.* Stanford, CA.: Stanford University Press.
Jenness, Diamond
1929 "Little Diomede Island, Bering Strait." *Geographical Review* 19(no.1):78-86.
Jesuit Missions
1927-1960 A monthly mission magazine.
"King Island Diary"
1943-59
"Kotzebue Diary"
1930-60
Krauss, Michael E.
1974 "Native Peoples and Languages of Alaska." Map (revised 1982) showing language spoken in each Native village. Alaska Native Language Center, University of Alaska, Fairbanks.
"Little Diomede Diary"
1936-55
Llorente, Segundo, S.J.
1969 *Jesuits in Alaska.* Portland, OR.: Graphic Arts Center.
Ménager, Francis M., S.J.
1937 "Father Tom's Kingdom." *Jesuit Missions* 11(no.8):200-01, 223.

Miller, Ed Mack
    1953 "Adventure is his parish." *Information* 67(no.1):5-10.
Morgan, Audrey and Frank
    1951 "Alaska's Russian Frontier: Little Diomede."
        National Geographic Magazine 99(no.4):551-62.
Muñoz, Juan
    1954 "Cliff Dwellers of the Bering Sea." *National Geographic Magazine*
        105(no.1):129-46.
Nelson, Richard K.
    1969 *Hunters of the Northern Ice.* Chicago and London:
        University of Chicago Press.
"Nome Diary"
    1901-60
O'Connor, Paul C., S.J.
    1943 "Alaskan Flyers to the Rescue." *Jesuit Missions*
        17(no.6):150-51, 167.
Potter, Jean
    1977 *The Flying North.* Sausalito, CA.: Comstock Editions, Inc.
Ray, Dorothy Jean
    1961 *Artists of the Tundra and the Sea.* Seattle and London:
        University of Washington Press.
    1975 *The Eskimos of Bering Strait, 1650-1898.* Seattle and London:
        University of Washington Press.
    1977 *Eskimo Art: Tradition and Innovation in North Alaska.*
        Seattle and London: University of Washington Press
Renner, Louis L., S.J.
        1975a "The Eskimos Return to King Island." *Catholic Digest*
            39(no.5):46-55.
        1975b "Return to King Island." *Alaska* 41(no.7):6-8.
        1975-76 "Catechizing the Vikings of Bering Strait."
            Eskimo 32(no. 10, New Series):5-20.
        1977-78 "Fr. Frederick Ruppert, S.J.: Martyr of Charity."
            Eskimo 34(no. 14, New Series):11-22.
        1979a "Farming at Holy Cross Mission." The Alaska Journal
            9(no.1):32-37.
        1979b *Pioneer Missionary to the Bering Strait Eskimos:*
            Bellarmine Lafortune, S.J. Portland, OR.:
            Binford & Mort. In collaboration with Dorothy Jean Ray.
        1980-81 "Fr. Aloysius Robaut, S.J.: Pioneer Missionary
            in Alaska." *Eskimo* 37(no. 20, New Series):5-16.

Roseberry, Cecil R.
1959 "Padre of the Arctic Ice." *American Weekly*, 18 January, pp. 1-2.
Ross, Frances A.
1959 "Father Thomas P. Cunningham, S.J." Typed manuscript.
Stefansson, Vilhjalmur
1921 *The Friendly Arctic.* New York: Macmillan.
Tate, Carrie
1943-44 "King Island Diary." Typed manuscript in Renner's possession.
Toner, Erwin J., S.J.
1958 "Arctic Priest, Technical Advisor for IGY Camp in Arctic Ocean."
        Oregon Jesuit 27(no.8):7, 13.
Weeks, Tim
1965 *Ice Island.* New York: John Day Co.

Index